Shakespeare
Explained

Julius
Caesar

JOSEPH
SOBRAN

mc **Marshall Cavendish**
Benchmark
New York

Series consultant: Richard Larkin

Marshall Cavendish
99 White Plains Road
Tarrytown, New York 10591
www.marshallcavendish.us

Library of Congress Cataloging-in-Publication Data
Sobran, Joseph.
Julius Caesar / by Joseph Sobran.
p. cm. — (Shakespeare explained)
Summary: "A literary analysis of the play Julius Caesar. Includes
information on the history and culture of Elizabethan England"—
Provided by publisher.
Includes bibliographical references and index.
ISBN 978-0-7614-3028-5
1. Shakespeare, William, 1564-1616. Julius Caesar—Juvenile literature.
I. Title.
PR2808.S63 2009
822.3'3—dc22
2008014404

Photo research by: Linda Sykes
The photographs in this book are used by permission and through the courtesy of: Royal
Shakespeare Theatre/Lebrecht Music and Arts: front cover; Semak/istockphoto, Neven
Mendrila/Shutterstock: 3; Raciro/istockphoto: 4; 38, 44, 100, 128; Art Parts RF: 6, 8, 13, 24, 25, 32;
Nik Wheeler/Corbis: 11; Portraitgalerie, Schloss Ambras, Innsbruck, Austria/Erich Lessing/ Art
Resource, NY: 18; AA World Travel Library/Alamy: 20; Hideo Kurihara/Alamy: 22; Corbis Sygma:
27; Andrew Fox/Corbis: 30; Folger Shakespeare Library/Art Resource, NY: 36-37; MGM/The
Kobal Collection: 43; Royal Shakespeare Company: 48, 65, 67; MGM/Photofest: 54; The Granger
Collection: 60, 85; Royal Shakespeare Theatre/Lebrecht Music and Arts: 62; Tristram Kenton/
Lebrecht Music and Arts: 72, 89; 2006 Charles Walker/Topfoto/The Image Works: 80; Photofest: 93;
Good Times Entertainment, 2004: 99.

Editor: Deborah Grahame
Publisher: Michelle Bisson
Art Director: Anahid Hamparian
Series Design: Kay Petronio

Printed in Malaysia

135642

Contents

SHAKESPEARE AND HIS WORLD . . . 4

1. SHAKESPEARE AND
JULIUS CAESAR . . . 36

2. THE PLAY'S THE THING . . . 42

3. A CLOSER LOOK . . . 98

CHRONOLOGY . . . 112

SOURCE NOTES . . . 114

GLOSSARY . . . 115

SUGGESTED ESSAY TOPICS . . . 119

TESTING YOUR MEMORY . . . 120

FURTHER INFORMATION . . . 122

BIBLIOGRAPHY . . . 124

INDEX . . . 125

Shakespeare and His World

WILLIAM SHAKESPEARE,

OFTEN NICKNAMED "THE BARD," IS, BEYOND ANY COMPARISON, THE MOST TOWERING NAME IN ENGLISH LITERATURE. MANY CONSIDER HIS PLAYS THE GREATEST EVER WRITTEN. HE STANDS OUT EVEN AMONG GENIUSES.

Yet the Bard is also closer to our hearts than lesser writers, and his tremendous reputation should neither intimidate us nor prevent us from enjoying the simple delights he offers in such abundance. It is as if he had written for each of us personally. As he himself put it, "One touch of nature makes the whole world kin."

Such tragedies as *Hamlet*, *Romeo and Juliet*, and *Macbeth* are world-famous, still performed on stage and in films. These and others have also been adapted for radio, television, opera, ballet, pantomime, novels, comic books, and other media. Two of the best ways to become familiar with them are to watch some of the many fine movies that have been made of them and to listen to recordings of them by some of the world's great actors.

Even Shakespeare's individual characters have a life of their own, like real historical figures. Hamlet is still regarded as the most challenging role ever written for an actor. Roughly as many whole books have been written about Hamlet, an imaginary character, as about actual historical figures such as Abraham Lincoln and Napoleon Bonaparte.

Shakespeare created an amazing variety of vivid characters. One of Shakespeare's most peculiar traits was that he loved his characters so much—even some of his villains and secondary or comic characters—that at times he let them run away with the play, stealing attention from his heroes and heroines.

So in *A Midsummer Night's Dream* audiences remember the absurd and lovable fool Bottom the Weaver better than the lovers who are the main characters. Romeo's friend Mercutio is more fiery and witty than Romeo himself; legend claims that Shakespeare said he had to kill Mercutio or Mercutio would have killed the play.

Shakespeare also wrote dozens of comedies and historical plays, as well as nondramatic poems. Although his tragedies are now regarded as his greatest works, he freely mixed them with comedy and history. And his sonnets are among the supreme love poems in the English language.

It is Shakespeare's mastery of the English language that keeps his words familiar to us today. Every literate person knows dramatic lines such as "Wherefore art thou Romeo?"; "My kingdom for a horse!"; "To be or not to be: that is the question"; "Friends, Romans, countrymen, lend me your ears"; and "What fools these mortals be!" Shakespeare's sonnets are noted for their sweetness: "Shall I compare thee to a summer's day?"

BEWARE THE IDES OF MARCH

SHAKESPEARE'S LANGUAGE

WITHOUT A DOUBT, SHAKESPEARE WAS THE GREATEST MASTER OF THE ENGLISH LANGUAGE WHO EVER LIVED. BUT JUST WHAT DOES THAT MEAN?

Shakespeare's vocabulary was huge, full of references to the Bible as well as Greek and Roman mythology. Yet his most brilliant phrases often combine very simple and familiar words:

"WHAT'S IN A NAME? THAT WHICH WE CALL A ROSE BY ANY OTHER NAME WOULD SMELL AS SWEET."

He has delighted countless millions of readers. And we know him only through his language. He has shaped modern English far more than any other writer.

Or, to put it in more personal terms, you probably quote his words several times every day without realizing it, even if you have never suspected that Shakespeare could be a source of pleasure to you.

So why do so many English-speaking readers find his language so difficult? It is our language, too, but it has changed so much that it is no longer quite the same language—nor a completely different one, either.

Shakespeare's English and ours overlap without being identical. He would have some difficulty understanding us, too! Many of our everyday words and phrases would baffle him.

Shakespeare, for example, would not know what we meant by a *car,* a *radio,* a *movie,* a *television,* a *computer,* or a *sitcom,* since these things did not even exist in his time. Our old-fashioned term *railroad train,* would be unimaginable to him, far in the distant future. We would have to explain to him (if we could) what *nuclear weapons, electricity,* and *democracy* are. He would also be a little puzzled by common expressions such as *high-tech, feel the heat, approval ratings, war criminal, judgmental,* and *whoopie cushion.*

So how can we call him "the greatest master of the English language"? It might seem as if he barely spoke English at all! (He would, however, recognize much of our dirty slang, even if he pronounced it slightly differently. His plays also contain many racial insults to Jews, Africans, Italians, Irish, and others. Today he would be called "insensitive.")

Many of the words of Shakespeare's time have become archaic. Words like *thou, thee, thy, thyself,* and *thine,* which were among the most common words in the language in Shakespeare's day, have all but disappeared today. We simply say *you* for both singular and plural, formal and familiar. Most other modern languages have kept their *thou.*

Sometimes the same words now have different meanings. We are apt to be misled by such simple, familiar words as *kind, wonderful, waste, just,* and *dear,* which he often uses in ways that differ from our usage.

Shakespeare also doesn't always use the words we expect to hear, the words that we ourselves would naturally use. When we might automatically say, "I beg your pardon" or just "Sorry," he might say, "I cry you mercy."

Often a glossary and footnotes will solve all three of these problems for us. But it is most important to bear in mind that Shakespeare was often hard for his first audiences to understand. Even in his own time his rich language was challenging. And this was deliberate. Shakespeare was inventing his own kind of English. It remains unique today.

A child doesn't learn to talk by using a dictionary. Children learn first by sheer immersion. We teach babies by pointing at things and saying their names. Yet the toddler always learns faster than we can teach! Even as babies we are geniuses. Dictionaries can help us later, when we already speak and read the language well (and learn more slowly).

So the best way to learn Shakespeare is not to depend on the footnotes and glossary too much, but instead to be like a baby: just get into the flow of the language. Go to performances of the plays or watch movies of them.

THE LANGUAGE HAS A MAGICAL WAY OF TEACHING ITSELF, IF WE LET IT. THERE IS NO REASON TO FEEL STUPID OR FRUSTRATED WHEN IT DOESN'T COME EASILY.

Hundreds of phrases have entered the English language from *Hamlet* alone, including "to hold, as t'were, the mirror up to nature"; "murder most foul"; "the thousand natural shocks that flesh is heir to"; "flaming youth"; "a countenance more in sorrow than in anger"; "the play's the thing"; "neither a borrower nor a lender be"; "in my mind's eye"; "something is rotten in the state of Denmark"; "alas, poor Yorick"; and "the lady doth protest too much, methinks."

From other plays we get the phrases "star-crossed lovers"; "what's in a name?"; "we have scotched the snake, not killed it"; "one fell swoop"; "it was Greek to me;" "I come to bury Caesar, not to praise him"; and "the most unkindest cut of all"—all these are among our household words. In fact, Shakespeare even gave us the expression "household words." No wonder his contemporaries marveled at his "fine filed phrase" and swooned at the "mellifluous and honey-tongued Shakespeare."

Shakespeare's words seem to combine music, magic, wisdom, and humor:

"THE COURSE OF TRUE LOVE NEVER DID RUN SMOOTH."

"HE JESTS AT SCARS THAT NEVER FELT A WOUND."

"THE FAULT, DEAR BRUTUS, IS NOT IN OUR STARS, BUT IN OURSELVES, THAT WE ARE UNDERLINGS."

"COWARDS DIE MANY TIMES BEFORE THEIR DEATHS; THE VALIANT NEVER TASTE OF DEATH BUT ONCE."

"NOT THAT I LOVED CAESAR LESS, BUT THAT I LOVED ROME MORE."

THERE ARE MORE THINGS IN HEAVEN AND EARTH, HORATIO, THAN ARE DREAMT OF IN YOUR PHILOSOPHY."

"BREVITY IS THE SOUL OF WIT."

"THERE'S A DIVINITY THAT SHAPES OUR ENDS, ROUGH-HEW THEM HOW WE WILL."

Four centuries after Shakespeare lived, to speak English is to quote him. His huge vocabulary and linguistic fertility are still astonishing. He has had a powerful effect on all of us, whether we realize it or not. We may wonder how it is even possible for a single human being to say so many memorable things.

Only the King James translation of the Bible, perhaps, has had a more profound and pervasive influence on the English language than Shakespeare. And, of course, the Bible was written by many authors over many centuries, and the King James translation, published in 1611, was the combined effort of many scholars.

EARLY LIFE

So who, exactly, was Shakespeare? Mystery surrounds his life, largely because few records were kept during his time. Some people have even doubted his identity, arguing that the real author of Shakespeare's plays must have been a man of superior formal education and wide experience. In a sense such doubts are a natural and understandable reaction to his rare, almost miraculous powers of expression, but some people feel that the doubts themselves show a lack of respect for the supremely human poet.

Most scholars agree that Shakespeare was born in the town of Stratford-upon-Avon in the county of Warwickshire, England, in April 1564. He was baptized, according to local church records, Gulielmus (William) Shakspere (the name was spelled in several different ways) on April 26 of that year. He was one of several children, most of whom died young.

His father, John Shakespeare (or Shakspere), was a glove maker and, at times, a town official. He was often in debt or being fined for unknown delinquencies, perhaps failure to attend church regularly. It is suspected that John was a "recusant" (secret and illegal) Catholic, but there is no proof.

Many scholars have found Catholic tendencies in Shakespeare's plays, but whether Shakespeare was Catholic or not we can only guess.

At the time of Shakespeare's birth, England was torn by religious controversy and persecution. The country had left the Roman Catholic Church during the reign of King Henry VIII, who had died in 1547. Two of Henry's children, Edward and Mary, ruled after his death. When his daughter Elizabeth I became queen in 1558, she upheld his claim that the monarch of England was also head of the English Church.

Did William attend the local grammar school? He was probably entitled to, given his father's prominence in Stratford, but again, we face a frustrating absence of proof, and many people of the time learned to read very well without schooling. If he went to the town school, he would also have learned the rudiments of Latin.

We know very little about the first half of William's life. In 1582, when he was eighteen, he married Anne Hathaway, eight years his senior. Their first daughter, Susanna, was born six months later. The following year they had twins, Hamnet and Judith.

At this point William disappears from the records again. By the early 1590s we find "William Shakespeare" in London, a member of the city's leading acting company, called the Lord Chamberlain's Men. Many of Shakespeare's greatest roles, we are told, were first performed by the company's star, Richard Burbage.

Curiously, the first work published under (and identified with) Shakespeare's name was not a play but a long erotic poem, *Venus and Adonis*, in 1593. It was dedicated to the young Earl of Southampton, Henry Wriothesley.

Venus and Adonis was a spectacular success, and Shakespeare was immediately hailed as a major poet. In 1594 he dedicated a longer, more serious poem to Southampton, *The Rape of Lucrece*. It was another hit, and for many years, these two poems were considered Shakespeare's greatest works, despite the popularity of his plays.

FRIENDS, ROMANS, COUNTRYMEN, LEND ME YOUR EARS

TODAY MOVIES, NOT LIVE PLAYS, ARE THE MORE POPULAR ART FORM. FORTUNATELY MOST OF SHAKESPEARE'S PLAYS HAVE BEEN FILMED, AND THE BEST OF THESE MOVIES OFFER AN EXCELLENT WAY TO MAKE THE BARD'S ACQUAINTANCE. RECENTLY, KENNETH BRANAGH HAS BECOME A RESPECTED CONVERTER OF SHAKESPEARE'S PLAYS INTO FILM.

Hamlet

Hamlet, Shakespeare's most famous play, has been well filmed several times. In 1948 Laurence Olivier won three Academy Awards—for best picture, best actor, and best director—for his version of the play. The film allowed him to show some of the magnetism that made him famous on the stage. Nobody spoke Shakespeare's lines more thrillingly.

The young Derek Jacobi played Hamlet in a 1980 BBC production of the play, with Patrick Stewart (now best known for *Star Trek, the Next Generation*) as the guilty king. Jacobi, like Olivier, has a gift for speaking the lines freshly; he never seems to be merely reciting the famous and familiar words. But whereas Olivier has animal passion, Jacobi is more intellectual. It is fascinating to compare the ways these two outstanding actors play Shakespeare's most complex character.

Franco Zeffirelli's 1990 *Hamlet*, starring Mel Gibson, is fascinating in a different way. Gibson, of course, is best known as an action hero, and he is not well suited to this supremely witty and introspective role, but Zeffirelli cuts the text drastically, and the result turns *Hamlet* into something that few people would have expected: a short, swift-moving action movie. Several of the other characters are brilliantly played.

Henry IV, Part One

The 1979 BBC Shakespeare series production does a commendable job in this straightforward approach to the play. Battle scenes are effective despite obvious restrictions in an indoor studio setting. Anthony Quayle gives jovial Falstaff a darker edge, and Tim Pigott-Smith's Hotspur is buoyed by some humor. Jon Finch plays King Henry IV with noble authority, and David Gwillim gives Hal a surprisingly successful transformation from boy prince to heir apparent.

Julius Caesar

No really good movie of *Julius Caesar* exists, but the 1953 film, with Marlon Brando as Mark Antony, will do. James Mason is a thoughtful Brutus, and John Gielgud, then ranked with Laurence Olivier among the greatest Shakespearean actors, plays the villainous Cassius. The film is rather dull, and Brando is out of place in a Roman toga, but it is still worth viewing.

Macbeth

Roman Polanski is best known as a director of thrillers and horror films, so it may seem natural that he should have done his 1971 *The Tragedy of Macbeth* as an often-gruesome slasher flick. But this is also one of the most vigorous of all Shakespeare films. Macbeth and his wife are played by Jon Finch and Francesca Annis, neither known for playing Shakespeare, but they are young and attractive in roles usually given to older actors, which gives the story a fresh flavor.

The Merchant of Venice

Once again the matchless Sir Laurence Olivier delivers a great performance as Shylock with his wife Joan Plowright as Portia in the 1974 TV film, adapted from the 1970 National Theater (of Britain) production. A 1980 BBC offering features Warren Mitchell as Shylock and Gemma Jones as Portia, with John Rhys-Davies as Salerio. The most recent production, starring Al Pacino as Shylock, Jeremy Irons as Antonio, and Joseph Fiennes as Bassanio, was filmed in Venice and released in 2004.

A Midsummer Night's Dream

Because of the prestige of his tragedies, we tend to forget how many comedies Shakespeare wrote—nearly twice the number of tragedies. Of these perhaps the most popular has always been the enchanting, atmospheric, and very silly masterpiece *A Midsummer Night's Dream*.

In more recent times several films have been made of *A Midsummer Night's Dream*. Among the more notable have been Max Reinhardt's 1935 black-and-white version, with Mickey Rooney (then a child star) as Puck

Of the several film versions, the one starring Kevin Kline as Bottom and Stanley Tucci as Puck, made in 1999 with nineteenth-century costumes and directed by Michael Hoffman, ranks among the finest, and is surely one of the most sumptuous to watch.

Othello

Orson Welles did a budget European version in 1952, now available as a restored DVD. Laurence Olivier's 1965 film performance is predictably remarkable, though it has been said that he would only approach the part by honoring, even emulating, Paul Robeson's definitive interpretation that ran on Broadway in 1943. (Robeson was the first black actor to play Othello, the Moor of Venice, and he did so to critical acclaim, though sadly his performance was never filmed.) Maggie Smith plays a formidable Desdemona opposite Olivier, and her youth and energy will surprise younger audiences who know her only from the Harry Potter films. Laurence Fishburne brilliantly portrayed Othello in the 1995 film, costarring with Kenneth Branagh as a surprisingly human Iago, though Irène Jacob's Desdemona was disappointingly weak.

Romeo and Juliet

This, the world's most famous love story, has been filmed many times, twice very successfully over the last generation. Franco Zeffirelli directed a hit version in 1968 with Leonard Whiting and the rapturously pretty Olivia Hussey, set in Renaissance Italy. Baz Luhrmann made a much more contemporary version, with a loud rock score, starring Leonardo Di Caprio and Claire Danes, in 1996.

It seems safe to say that Shakespeare would have preferred Zeffirelli's movie, with its superior acting and rich, romantic, sun-drenched Italian scenery.

The Tempest

A 1960 Hallmark Hall of Fame production featured Maurice Evans as Prospero, Lee Remick as Miranda, Roddy McDowall as Ariel, and Richard Burton as Caliban. The special effects are primitive and the costumes are ludicrous, but it moves along at a fast pace. Another TV version aired in 1998 and was nominated for a Golden Globe. Peter Fonda played Gideon Prosper, and Katherine Heigl played his daughter Miranda Prosper. Sci-Fi fans may already know that the classic 1956 film *Forbidden Planet* is modeled on themes and characters from the play.

Twelfth Night

Trevor Nunn adapted the play for the 1996 film he also directed in a rapturous Edwardian setting, with big names like Helena Bonham Carter, Richard E. Grant, Imogen Stubbs, and Ben Kingsley as Feste. A 2003 film set in modern Britain provides an interesting multicultural experience; it features an Anglo-Indian cast with Parminder Nagra (*Bend It Like Beckham*) playing Viola. For the truly intrepid viewer, a twelve-minute silent film made in 1910 does a fine job of capturing the play through visual gags and over-the-top gesturing.

THESE FILMS HAVE BEEN SELECTED FOR SEVERAL QUALITIES: APPEAL AND ACCESSIBILITY TO MODERN AUDIENCES, EXCELLENCE IN ACTING, PACING, VISUAL BEAUTY, AND, OF COURSE, FIDELITY TO SHAKESPEARE. THEY ARE THE MOTION PICTURES WE JUDGE MOST LIKELY TO HELP STUDENTS UNDERSTAND THE SOURCE OF THE BARD'S LASTING POWER.

Today we sometimes speak of "live entertainment." In Shakespeare's day, of course, all entertainment was live, because recordings, films, television, and radio did not yet exist. Even printed books were a novelty.

In fact, most communication in those days was difficult. Transportation was not only difficult but slow, chiefly by horse and boat. Most people were illiterate peasants who lived on farms that they seldom left; cities grew up along waterways and were subject to frequent plagues that could wipe out much of the population within weeks.

Money—in coin form, not paper—was scarce and hardly existed outside the cities. By today's standards, even the rich were poor. Life

ELIZABETH I, A GREAT PATRON OF POETRY AND THE THEATER, WROTE SONNETS AND TRANSLATED CLASSIC WORKS.

was precarious. Most children died young, and famine or disease might kill anyone at any time. Everyone was familiar with death. Starvation was not rare or remote, as it is to most of us today. Medical care was poor and might kill as many people as it healed.

This was the grim background of Shakespeare's theater during the reign of Queen Elizabeth I, who ruled from 1558 until her death in 1603. During that period England was also torn by religious conflict, often violent, among Roman Catholics who were loyal to the Pope, adherents of the Church of England who were loyal to the queen, and the Puritans who would take over the country in the revolution of 1642.

Under these conditions, most forms of entertainment were luxuries that were out of most people's reach. The only way to hear music was to be in the actual physical presence of singers or musicians with their instruments, which were primitive by our standards.

One brutal form of entertainment, popular in London, was bear-baiting. A bear was blinded and chained to a stake, where fierce dogs called mastiffs were turned loose to tear him apart. The theaters had to compete with the bear gardens, as they were called, for spectators.

The Puritans, or radical Protestants, objected to bear-baiting and tried to ban it. Despite their modern reputation, the Puritans were anything but conservative. Conservative people, attached to old customs, hated them. They seemed to upset everything. (Many of America's first settlers, such as the Pilgrims who came over on the *Mayflower*, were dissidents who were fleeing the Church of England.)

Plays were extremely popular, but they were primitive, too. They had to be performed outdoors in the afternoon because of the lack of indoor lighting. Often the "theater" was only an enclosed courtyard. Probably the versions of Shakespeare's plays that we know today were not used in full, but shortened to about two hours for actual performance.

But eventually more regular theaters were built, featuring a raised stage extending into the audience. Poorer spectators (illiterate "groundlings") stood on the ground around it, at times exposed to rain and snow. Wealthier people sat in raised tiers above. Aside from some costumes, there were few props or special effects and almost no scenery. Much had to be imagined: Whole battles might be represented by a few actors with swords. Thunder might be simulated by rattling a sheet of tin offstage.

The plays were far from realistic and, under the conditions of the time, could hardly try to be. Above the rear of the main stage was a small balcony. (It was this balcony from which Juliet spoke to Romeo.) Ghosts and witches might appear by entering through a trapdoor in the stage floor.

Unlike the modern theater, Shakespeare's Globe Theater—he describes it as "this wooden O"—had no curtain separating the stage from the audience. This allowed intimacy between the players and the spectators.

THE RECONSTRUCTED GLOBE THEATER WAS COMPLETED IN 1997 AND IS LOCATED IN LONDON, JUST 200 YARDS (183 METERS) FROM THE SITE OF THE ORIGINAL.

BUT FOR MY OWN PART, IT WAS GREEK TO ME.

The spectators probably reacted rowdily to the play, not listening in reverent silence. After all they had come to have fun! And few of them were scholars. Again, a play had to amuse people who could not read.

The lines of plays were written and spoken in prose or, more often, in a form of verse called iambic pentameter (ten syllables with five stresses per line). There was no attempt at modern realism. Only males were allowed on the stage, so some of the greatest women's roles ever written had to be played by boys or men. (The same is true, by the way, of the ancient Greek theater.)

Actors had to be versatile, skilled not only in acting, but also in fencing, singing, dancing, and acrobatics. Within its limitations, the theater offered a considerable variety of spectacles.

Plays were big business, not yet regarded as high art, sponsored by important and powerful people (the queen loved them as much as the groundlings did). The London acting companies also toured and performed in the provinces. When plagues struck London, the government might order the theaters to be closed to prevent the spread of disease among crowds. (They remained empty for nearly two years from 1593 to 1594.)

As the theater became more popular, the Puritans grew as hostile to it as they were to bear-baiting. Plays, like books, were censored by the government, and the Puritans fought to increase restrictions, eventually banning any mention of God and other sacred topics on the stage.

In 1642 the Puritans shut down all the theaters in London, and in 1644 they had the Globe demolished. The theaters remained closed until Charles's son King Charles II was restored to the throne in 1660 and the hated Puritans were finally vanquished.

But, by then, the tradition of Shakespeare's theater had been fatally interrupted. His plays remained popular, but they were often rewritten by inferior dramatists and it was many years before they were performed (again) as he had originally written them.

THE ROYAL SHAKESPEARE THEATER, IN STRATFORD-UPON-AVON, WAS CLOSED IN 2007. A NEWLY DESIGNED INTERIOR WITH A 1000-SEAT AUDITORIUM WILL BE COMPLETED IN 2010.

Today, of course, the plays are performed both in theaters and in films, sometimes in costumes of the period (ancient Rome for *Julius Caesar*, medieval England for *Henry V*), sometimes in modern dress (*Richard III* has recently been reset in England in the 1930s).

PLAYS

In the England of Queen Elizabeth I, plays were enjoyed by all classes of people, but they were not yet respected as a serious form of art.

Shakespeare's plays began to appear in print in individual, or "quarto," editions in 1594, but none of these bore his name until 1598. Although his tragedies are now ranked as his supreme achievements, his name was first associated with comedies and with plays about English history.

The dates of Shakespeare's plays are notoriously hard to determine. Few performances of them were documented; some were not printed until decades after they first appeared on the stage. Mainstream scholars generally place most of the comedies and histories in the 1590s, admitting that this time frame is no more than a widely accepted estimate.

The three parts of *King Henry VI*, culminating in a fourth part, *Richard III*, deal with the long and complex dynastic struggle or civil wars known as the Wars of the Roses (1455–1487), one of England's most turbulent periods. Today it is not easy to follow the plots of these plays.

It may seem strange to us that a young playwright should have written such demanding works early in his career, but they were evidently very popular with the Elizabethan public. Of the four, only *Richard III*, with its wonderfully villainous starring role, is still often performed.

Even today, one of Shakespeare's early comedies, *The Taming of the Shrew*, remains a crowd-pleaser. (It has enjoyed success in a 1999 film adaptation, *10 Things I Hate About You* with Heath Ledger and Julia Stiles.)

THE "REAL" SHAKESPEARE

AROUND 1850 DOUBTS STARTED TO SURFACE ABOUT WHO HAD ACTUALLY WRITTEN SHAKESPEARE'S PLAYS, CHIEFLY BECAUSE MANY OTHER AUTHORS, SUCH AS MARK TWAIN, THOUGHT THE PLAYS' AUTHOR WAS TOO WELL EDUCATED AND KNOWLEDGEABLE TO HAVE BEEN THE MODESTLY SCHOOLED MAN FROM STRATFORD.

Who, then, was the real author? Many answers have been given, but the three leading candidates are Francis Bacon, Christopher Marlowe, and Edward de Vere, Earl of Oxford.

Francis Bacon (1561-1626)

Bacon was a distinguished lawyer, scientist, philosopher, and essayist. Many considered him one of the great geniuses of his time, capable of any literary achievement, though he wrote little poetry and, as far as we know, no dramas. When people began to suspect that "Shakespeare" was only a pen name, he seemed like a natural candidate. But his writing style was vastly different from the style of the plays.

Christopher Marlowe (1564–1593)

Marlowe wrote several excellent tragedies in a style much like that of the Shakespeare tragedies, though without the comic blend. But he was reportedly killed in a mysterious incident in 1593, before most of the Bard's plays existed. Could his death have been faked? Is it possible that he lived on for decades in hiding, writing under a pen name? This is what his advocates contend.

Edward de Vere, Earl of Oxford (1550–1604)

Oxford is now the most popular and plausible alternative to the lad from Stratford. He had a high reputation as a poet and playwright in his day, but his life was full of scandal. That controversial life seems to match what the poet says about himself in the sonnets, as well as many events in the plays (especially *Hamlet*). However, he died in 1604, and most scholars believe this rules him out as the author of plays that were published after that date.

THE GREAT MAJORITY OF EXPERTS REJECT THESE AND ALL OTHER ALTERNATIVE CANDIDATES, STICKING WITH THE TRADITIONAL VIEW, AFFIRMED IN THE 1623 FIRST FOLIO OF THE PLAYS, THAT THE AUTHOR WAS THE MAN FROM STRATFORD. THAT REMAINS THE SAFEST POSITION TO TAKE, UNLESS STARTLING NEW EVIDENCE TURNS UP, WHICH, AT THIS LATE DATE, SEEMS HIGHLY UNLIKELY.

The story is simple: The enterprising Petruchio resolves to marry a rich young woman, Katherina Minola, for her wealth, despite her reputation for having a bad temper. Nothing she does can discourage this dauntless suitor, and the play ends with Kate becoming a submissive wife. It is all the funnier for being unbelievable.

With *Romeo and Juliet* the Bard created his first enduring triumph. This tragedy of "star-crossed lovers" from feuding families is known around the world. Even people with only the vaguest knowledge of Shakespeare are often aware of this universally beloved story. It has inspired countless similar stories and adaptations, such as the hit musical *West Side Story*.

By the mid-1590s Shakespeare was successful and prosperous, a partner in the Lord Chamberlain's Men. He was rich enough to buy New Place, one of the largest houses in his hometown of Stratford.

Yet, at the peak of his good fortune, came the worst sorrow of his life: Hamnet, his only son, died in August 1596 at the age of eleven, leaving nobody to carry on his family name, which was to die out with his two daughters.

Our only evidence of his son's death is a single line in the parish burial register. As far as we know, this crushing loss left no mark on Shakespeare's work. As far as his creative life shows, it was as if nothing had happened. His silence about his grief may be the greatest puzzle of his mysterious life, although, as we shall see, others remain.

During this period, according to traditional dating (even if it must be somewhat hypothetical), came the torrent of Shakespeare's mightiest works. Among these was another quartet of English history plays, this one centering on the legendary King Henry IV, including *Richard II* and the two parts of *Henry IV*.

Then came a series of wonderful romantic comedies: *Much Ado About Nothing*, *As You Like It*, and *Twelfth Night*.

ACTOR JOSEPH FIENNES PORTRAYED THE BARD IN THE 1998 FILM *SHAKESPEARE IN LOVE*, DIRECTED BY JOHN MADDEN.

In 1598 the clergyman Francis Meres, as part of a larger work, hailed Shakespeare as the English Ovid, supreme in love poetry as well as drama. "The Muses would speak with Shakespeare's fine filed phrase," Meres wrote, "if they would speak English." He added praise of Shakespeare's "sugared sonnets among his private friends." It is tantalizing; Meres seems to know something of the poet's personal life, but he gives us no hard information. No wonder biographers are frustrated.

Next the Bard returned gloriously to tragedy with *Julius Caesar*. In the play Caesar has returned to Rome in great popularity after his military triumphs. Brutus and several other leading senators, suspecting that Caesar means to make himself king, plot to assassinate him. Midway through the play, after the assassination, comes one of Shakespeare's most famous scenes. Brutus speaks at Caesar's funeral. But then Caesar's friend Mark Antony delivers a powerful attack on the conspirators, inciting the mob to fury. Brutus and the others, forced to flee Rome, die in the ensuing civil war. In the end the spirit of Caesar wins after all. If Shakespeare had written nothing after *Julius Caesar*, he would still have been remembered as one of the greatest playwrights of all time. But his supreme works were still to come.

Only Shakespeare could have surpassed *Julius Caesar*, and he did so with *Hamlet* (usually dated about 1600). King Hamlet of Denmark has died, apparently bitten by a poisonous snake. Claudius, his brother, has married the dead king's widow, Gertrude, and become the new king, to the disgust and horror of Prince Hamlet. The ghost of old Hamlet appears to young Hamlet, reveals that he was actually poisoned by Claudius, and demands revenge. Hamlet accepts this as his duty, but cannot bring himself to kill his hated uncle. What follows is Shakespeare's most brilliant and controversial plot.

The story of *Hamlet* is set against the religious controversies of the Bard's time. Is the ghost in hell or purgatory? Is Hamlet Catholic or Protestant? Can revenge ever be justified? We are never really given the answers to such questions. But the play reverberates with them.

THE KING'S MEN

In 1603 Queen Elizabeth I died, and King James VI of Scotland became King James I of England. He also became the patron of Shakespeare's acting company, so the Lord Chamberlain's Men became the King's Men. From this point on, we know less of Shakespeare's life in London than in Stratford, where he kept acquiring property.

In the later years of the sixteenth century Shakespeare had been a rather elusive figure in London, delinquent in paying taxes. From 1602 to 1604 he lived, according to his own later testimony, with a French immigrant family named Mountjoy. After 1604 there is no record of any London residence for Shakespeare, nor do we have any reliable recollection of him or his whereabouts by others. As always, the documents leave much to be desired.

Nearly as great as *Hamlet* is *Othello*, and many regard *King Lear*, the heartbreaking tragedy about an old king and his three daughters, as Shakespeare's supreme tragedy. Shakespeare's shortest tragedy, *Macbeth*, tells the story of a Scottish lord and his wife who plot to murder the king of Scotland to gain the throne for themselves. *Antony and Cleopatra*, a sequel to *Julius Caesar*, depicts the aging Mark Antony in love with the enchanting queen of Egypt. *Coriolanus*, another Roman tragedy, is the poet's least popular masterpiece.

SONNETS AND THE END

The year 1609 saw the publication of Shakespeare's sonnets. Of these 154 puzzling love poems, the first 126 are addressed to a handsome young man, unnamed, but widely believed to be the Earl of Southampton; the rest concern a dark woman, also unidentified. These mysteries are still debated by scholars.

Near the end of his career Shakespeare turned to comedy again, but it was a comedy of a new and more serious kind. Magic plays a large role in these late plays. For example, in *The Tempest*, the exiled duke of Milan, Prospero, uses magic to defeat his enemies and bring about a final reconciliation.

According to the most commonly accepted view, Shakespeare, not yet fifty, retired to Stratford around 1610. He died prosperous in 1616, and left a will that divided his goods, with a famous provision leaving his wife "my second-best bed." He was buried in the chancel of the parish church, under a tombstone bearing a crude rhyme:

> GOOD FRIEND, FOR JESUS SAKE FORBEARE
> TO DIG THE DUST ENCLOSED HERE.
> BLEST BE THE MAN THAT SPARES THESE STONES,
> AND CURSED BE HE THAT MOVES MY BONES.

This epitaph is another hotly debated mystery: Did the great poet actually compose these lines himself?

SHAKESPEARE'S GRAVE IN HOLY TRINITY CHURCH, STRATFORD-UPON-AVON. HIS WIFE ANNE HATHAWAY, IS BURIED BESIDE HIM.

In 1623 Shakespeare's colleagues of the King's Men produced a large volume of the plays (excluding the sonnets and other poems) titled *The Comedies, Histories, and Tragedies of Mr. William Shakespeare* with a woodcut portrait—the only known portrait—of the Bard. As a literary monument it is priceless, containing our only texts of half the plays; as a source of biographical information it is severely disappointing, giving not even the dates of Shakespeare's birth and death.

Ben Jonson, then England's poet laureate, supplied a long prefatory poem saluting Shakespeare as the equal of the great classical Greek tragedians Aeschylus, Sophocles, and Euripides, adding that "He was not of an age, but for all time."

Some would later denigrate Shakespeare. His reputation took more than a century to conquer Europe, where many regarded him as semi-barbarous. His works were not translated before 1740. Jonson himself, despite his personal affection, would deprecate "idolatry" of the Bard. For a time Jonson himself was considered more "correct" than Shakespeare, and possibly the superior artist.

But Jonson's generous verdict is now the whole world's. Shakespeare was not merely of his own age, "but for all time."

HE DOTH BESTRIDE THE NARROW WORLD LIKE A COLOSSUS

allegory—a story in which characters and events stand for general moral truths. Shakespeare never uses this form simply, but his plays are full of allegorical elements.

alliteration—repetition of one or more initial sounds, especially consonants, as in the saying "through thick and thin," or in Julius Caesar's statement, "veni, vidi, vici."

allusion—a reference, especially when the subject referred to is not actually named, but is unmistakably hinted at.

aside—a short speech in which a character speaks to the audience, unheard by other characters on the stage.

comedy—a story written to amuse, using devices such as witty dialogue (high comedy) or silly physical movement (low comedy). Most of Shakespeare's comedies were romantic comedies, incorporating lovers who endure separations, misunderstandings, and other obstacles but who are finally united in a happy resolution.

deus ex machine—an unexpected, artificial resolution to a play's convoluted plot. Literally, "god out of a machine."

dialogue—speech that takes place among two or more characters.

diction—choice of words for tone. A speech's diction may be dignified (as when a king formally addresses his court), comic (as when the ignorant gravediggers debate whether Ophelia deserves a religious funeral), vulgar, romantic, or whatever the dramatic occasion requires. Shakespeare was a master of diction.

Elizabethan—having to do with the reign of Queen Elizabeth I, from 1558 until her death in 1603. This is considered the most famous period in the history of England, chiefly because of Shakespeare and other noted authors (among them Sir Philip Sidney, Edmund Spenser, and Christopher Marlowe). It was also an era of military glory, especially the defeat of the huge Spanish Armada in 1588.

Globe—the Globe Theater housed Shakespeare's acting company, the Lord Chamberlain's Men (later known as the King's Men). Built in 1598, it caught fire and burned down during a performance of *Henry VIII* in 1613.

hyperbole—an excessively elaborate exaggeration used to create special emphasis or a comic effect, as in Montague's remark that his son Romeo's sighs are "adding to clouds more clouds" in *Romeo and Juliet.*

irony—a discrepancy between what a character says and what he or she truly believes, what is expected to happen and what really happens, or between what a character says and what others understand.

metaphor—a figure of speech in which one thing is identified with another, such as when Hamlet calls his father a "fair mountain." (See also **simile**.)

monologue—a speech delivered by a single character.

motif—a recurrent theme or image, such as disease in *Hamlet* or moonlight in *A Midsummer Night's Dream*.

oxymoron—a phrase that combines two contradictory terms, as in the phrase "sounds of silence" or Hamlet's remark, "I must be cruel only to be kind."

personification—imparting personality to something impersonal ("the sky wept"); giving human qualities to an idea or an inanimate object, as in the saying "love is blind."

pun—a playful treatment of words that sound alike, or are exactly the same, but have different meanings. In *Romeo and Juliet* Mercutio says, after being fatally wounded, "Ask for me tomorrow and you shall find me a grave man." "Grave" could mean either a place of burial or serious.

simile—a figure of speech in which one thing is compared to another, usually using the word *like* or *as*. (See also **metaphor**.)

soliloquy—a speech delivered by a single character, addressed to the audience. The most famous are those of Hamlet, but Shakespeare uses this device frequently to tell us his characters' inner thoughts.

symbol—a visible thing that stands for an invisible quality, as poison in *Hamlet* stands for evil and treachery.

syntax—sentence structure or grammar. Shakespeare displays amazing variety of syntax, from the sweet simplicity of his songs to the clotted fury of his great tragic heroes, who can be very difficult to understand at a first hearing. These effects are deliberate; if we are confused, it is because Shakespeare means to confuse us.

theme—the abstract subject or message of a work of art, such as revenge in *Hamlet* or overweening ambition in *Macbeth*.

tone—the style or approach of a work of art. The tone of *A Midsummer Night's Dream*, set by the lovers, Bottom's crew, and the fairies, is light and sweet. The tone of *Macbeth*, set by the witches, is dark and sinister.

tragedy—a story that traces a character's fall from power, sanity, or privilege. Shakespeare's well-known tragedies include *Hamlet, Macbeth,* and *Othello.*

tragicomedy—a story that combines elements of both tragedy and comedy, moving a heavy plot through twists and turns to a happy ending.

verisimilitude—having the appearance of being real or true.

understatement—a statement expressing less than intended, often with an ironic or comic intention; the opposite of hyperbole.

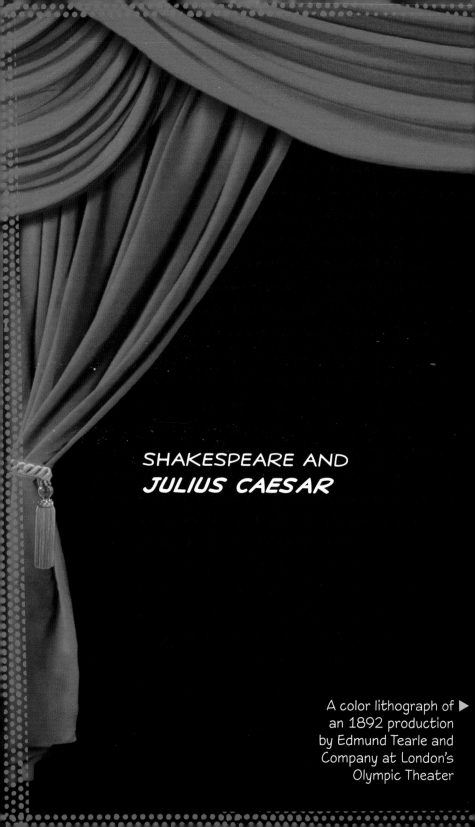

SHAKESPEARE AND
JULIUS CAESAR

A color lithograph of ▶
an 1892 production
by Edmund Tearle and
Company at London's
Olympic Theater

EDMUND TEARLE and COM...

Julius Cæsar

OLYMPIC THEATRE

66929 66929

Chapter
One

CHAPTER ONE

Shakespeare and Julius Caesar

JULIUS CAESAR IS AMONG THE MOST OFTEN QUOTED WORKS IN THE ENGLISH LANGUAGE; THE MOST RECENT EDITION OF *BARTLETT'S FAMILIAR QUOTATIONS* HAS SEVENTY-FOUR SELECTIONS FROM *JULIUS CAESAR* ALONE. SO IT IS A MEASURE OF SHAKESPEARE'S GENIUS THAT FEW SCHOLARS WOULD RANK THIS MEMORABLE MASTERPIECE AMONG HIS GREATEST PLAYS.

In fact this play is usually placed rather low among Shakespeare's tragedies. It lacks several of the elements that are typical of his work: a single tremendous hero, a great female character, lyrical verse, rich humor, a splendid vocabulary, and overpowering emotional impact. A. C. Bradley does not include it among the Bard's four supreme tragedies in his seminal book *Shakespearean Tragedy* (a profound study of *Hamlet*, *Othello*, *King Lear*, and *Macbeth*).

But this is not to say that *Julius Caesar* has no distinctive excellence; on the contrary, it stands out from all the drama before it.

European tragedy had traditionally been a simple tale of the misfortunes of a great man—typically, the fall of a king, often a tyrant who fully deserved his ruin. Many playwrights had followed this popular formula. The basic conflict was external, a cautionary tale about the vicissitudes of fate and fortune (Fortune's wheel was the old symbol of man's ever-changing luck).

With *Julius Caesar*, however, Shakespeare was developing a new kind of tragedy, one in which he has no rival: that of the inwardly divided hero, tormented by his conscience, revealing his internal conflict in one of the Bard's favorite dramatic devices, the soliloquy. This psychological conflict within the hero's soul mirrors and intensifies the outer one he confronts. Thanks in great part to the soliloquy, this poet who lived over four centuries before us gives the uncanny impression of knowing us better than we know ourselves and expressing our innermost thoughts and feelings more aptly than we could.

In Shakespearean tragedy the hero is never purely evil; there is always something about him that commands our interest, respect, and usually our sympathy. His own flaws cause his downfall; but still, we are not made to feel that this is simple justice. As Bradley says, we feel that someone both very human and very great, someone who is like ourselves yet much larger than we are, has been destroyed. Even if (like Macbeth) he has brought his

THE FAULT, DEAR BRUTUS, IS NOT IN OUR STARS, BUT IN OURSELVES

fate on himself by committing terrible crimes, we also feel a sense of waste and loss. Whatever evil he may have chosen to do, something of his natural dignity continues to exist even in his death. Shakespeare's real subject, we always feel, is human grandeur itself.

No wonder Shakespeare is still loved all over the world! Cassius is half-right when he joyfully predicts, over Caesar's bleeding corpse:

> HOW MANY AGES HENCE
> SHALL THIS OUR LOFTY SCENE BE ACTED OVER
> IN STATES UNBORN AND ACCENTS YET UNKNOWN!

At the time of these events, England was still far from being a state, and the English language did not yet exist. When Shakespeare wrote, Europeans had only recently discovered America, and English was not yet spoken here. Cassius and his fellow assassins are of course badly mistaken to imagine that posterity will honor them for saving liberty from tyranny—indeed Caesar's death helped destroy liberty in Rome and led to an era of terrifying tyrants—but it is true that the world has never forgotten the bloody deed committed on the Ides of March.

Some of the actual results of Caesar's assassination may be gathered from accounts of his successors, such as Caligula, Nero, and Domitian; see *The Twelve Caesars* by Suetonius—perhaps the most blood-curdling book of gossip ever written. Literate men of Shakespeare's generation were well aware of this history and had no illusions that the assassination of Julius Caesar had saved Rome's liberty and freedom. Many of them saw Queen Elizabeth I as a tyrant like Caesar, but it was not easy to decide what should be done about her; history is always full of lessons for the present, but they are seldom simple.

Julius Caesar also reflects the old debate among philosophers and

Christian theologians about whether, and under what conditions, the assassination of a ruler could be justified for the common good of the larger society. But Shakespeare's Brutus seems unaware that some of his fellow conspirators, such as Cassius, want to kill Caesar not for the common good, but for private revenge or to satisfy their own spite.

Brutus thinks he can save Rome from tyranny by emulating his legendary ancestor Lucius Junius Brutus, who had expelled the oppressive ruling family of the Tarquins from Rome (for a short summary of these events, see the prose prologue to *The Rape of Lucrece*); this, however, turns out to be his tragic error.

YOND' CASSIUS HAS A LEAN AND HUNGRY LOOK

THE PLAY'S THE THING

- OVERVIEW AND ANALYSIS

- LIST OF CHARACTERS

- ANALYSIS OF MAJOR CHARACTERS

A lobby card of the ▶
MGM 1953 film
directed by Joseph L.
Mankiewicz

CHAPTER
TWO

The Play's the Thing

ACT I, SCENE 1

OVERVIEW

Like so many of Shakespeare's plays, *Julius Caesar* begins with festivity.
The people of Rome—most of them, anyway—are rejoicing.

Flavius and Marullus are Rome's two tribunes—the representatives
of the common people. But today, on the feast of Lupercal, February 15,
they are furious with the city's tradesmen, who, instead of minding their
shops as required by the law, are out in the streets dressed in their finest
clothes to celebrate the victory of Julius Caesar over Pompey in the civil
war that has seen Pompey slain. As the commoners disperse, shamed by

the tribunes' scoldings, Flavius and Marullus resolve to strip away any ornaments that decorate images of Caesar.

ANALYSIS

How is Shakespeare going to build suspense about the most famous assassination of all time? This is one of the most daunting challenges any dramatist has ever faced. Note his artistry. At once he establishes tension between the two tribunes and the plebeians they supposedly represent. The two tribunes are still loyal to the memory of the defeated Pompey; the common people are already devoted to their new favorite, the conquering Caesar. The Bard readies our minds for a clash between partisans of the old order and the champions of the new.

ACT I, SCENE 2

OVERVIEW

Caesar orders his wife, Calpurnia, to let Antony touch her when he runs his race in the course of the Lupercalian festival. He says that, according to tradition, this may cure her infertility and give him a male heir.

Antony agrees to this. Just then a soothsayer (fortune-teller) steps forth from the crowd to warn Caesar, "Beware the Ides of March." Caesar dismisses the man as a "dreamer."

As Caesar and his followers leave, Cassius takes Brutus aside. He remarks that Brutus has seemed cool to him lately. Brutus apologizes, explaining that any coolness he has seemed to show toward Cassius merely reflects his own internal emotional turmoil.

Guessing at what is troubling Brutus, Cassius tells him that many of the most respected men in Rome, having the highest regard for him, wish he could see himself as he is at this critical moment in Roman history. Brutus and Cassius hear the people shout. Brutus quickly remarks, "I do fear the people/Choose Caesar for their king."

Seizing on the word *fear*, Cassius replies that Brutus must object to the idea. Brutus says that is true, despite his personal love for his old friend Caesar. But if he has to choose between honor and death, he will decide without fear.

Cassius says he has no doubt of Brutus's honor; in fact honor is what he now wants to discuss. Here he recalls a pair of incidents that revealed Caesar's weaknesses: once when he himself had to save Caesar from drowning in the Tiber, and on another occasion in Spain when the feverish Caesar, in the voice of a sick girl, begged Titinius for something to drink. Cassius marvels that the Romans can now revere this pathetic man as a god.

Again the people are heard cheering Caesar. Cassius is revolted by their adulation. Why should Caesar command more respect than anyone else—such as Brutus, for example? Cassius notes that one of Brutus's ancestors, also named Brutus, is still renowned for fearlessly vanquishing a tyrant (Tarquin the Proud, the villain of Shakespeare's long poem *The Rape of Lucrece*).

Brutus understands what Cassius is driving at—Caesar's assassination—and promises to weigh it and discuss it later. Meanwhile the games are over and Caesar returns with Calpurnia, Antony, and others. Caesar looks angry. He tells Antony to distrust the "lean and hungry" Cassius, who "thinks too much," rarely smiles, dislikes plays and music, and seems dangerous. When Antony tells him not to fear Cassius, Caesar insists that he fears nobody, but if he were capable of fear, Cassius is the one man he would surely avoid.

Brutus asks the sour Casca, who has watched the day's events, to describe what he has seen. Casca scornfully recounts the way Antony three times offered Caesar a crown, to the cheers of the multitude; and though Caesar refused it each time, he did so with increasing reluctance. The cynical Casca, with rude and blunt humor, has no doubt of Caesar's hunger for power. Casca will be part of the conspiracy to kill Caesar.

After Casca leaves, Brutus once more promises Cassius that he will consider what they have indirectly discussed: the assassination of Caesar.

Left alone Cassius reflects that the honorable but too trusting Brutus will be a great asset to the conspiracy. He is frank about his own intention to use Brutus's nobility of mind for evil purposes: "For who so firm that cannot be seduced?" Brutus, known for his strict honor and love of Caesar, will give the plot against Caesar respectability. Besides, Caesar himself, who has many enemies, loves and trusts Brutus. That night Cassius will send Brutus forged letters, seemingly written by various citizens, urging him to join the plot.

ANALYSIS

We meet Caesar; his infertile wife, Calpurnia; his friend Antony; the sinister Cassius; and the noble Brutus, who loves Caesar but fears his ambition. A soothsayer warns Caesar to "Beware the Ides of March" (March 15); Caesar tries to dismiss him as a "dreamer." This long scene is an excellent example of Shakespeare's skill in exposition, imparting as much information as possible while preparing us for the action to come.

Notice the huge challenge Shakespeare faces: The audience knows it is about to see a reenactment of one of the most famous historical events of all time, the murder of Julius Caesar. How is Shakespeare going to create suspense about something that everyone in the theater knows we are going to watch? He has his work cut out for him, but as we will see, the world's supreme dramatist rises to the occasion. (Then he will surpass it with the greatest oration ever written.)

CALPURNIA (CHRISTINA GREATREX) AND CAESAR (BREWSTER MASON) APPEAR IN ACT I OF THE ROYAL SHAKESPEARE COMPANY'S (RSC'S) 1968 PRODUCTION.

Notice also Shakespeare's wondrous character portrayal of Caesar. Although Caesar is the play's title character, he speaks fewer than three dozen lines in this scene. We will see him only once more before the scene in which he is slain; and yet he is the most vivid and colorful figure in the story, nearly every one of his lines unforgettable. (*Julius Caesar* is barely half as long as *Hamlet*; the two plays' title roles could hardly be in stronger contrast, one almost tiny, the other one of the longest speaking parts in all of the world's dramatic literature. Yet both characters seem to possess our imaginations from the first words they speak.)

Cassius manages Brutus's emotions superbly. First he says he will merely speak as his friend's "glass," or "mirror," showing him only what is already within him—namely, the love of honor. But as the scene progresses, he also appeals to Brutus's self-importance, vanity, and pride in his ancestors, likening Caesar to the kings whom the ancient Brutus once drove out of Rome. Brutus has none of Cassius's envy or resentment against Caesar, but Cassius knows that there are other ways by which Brutus may be "seduced." When Cassius has finished, Brutus is ready to join the conspiracy to assassinate Caesar.

ACT I, SCENE 3

OVERVIEW

Nearly a month later, on the night of March 14, Casca and the great orator Cicero, famed for his wisdom and eloquence, meet during a violent storm. Terrifying signs fill the skies and streets of Rome. Casca wonders whether there is "a civil strife in heaven" or if overbearing men have provoked the gods to destroy them. He adds that he has seen other wondrous things: A slave's raised hand has burst into flames without suffering pain, a lion has appeared near the Capitol, ghastly women have sworn that they saw men on fire walking the streets, and owls have shrieked at noon. It all seems quite unnatural. Cicero comments that men may misinterpret such apparent marvels:

> MEN MAY CONSTRUE THINGS AFTER THEIR FASHION, CLEAN FROM THE PURPOSE OF THE THINGS THEMSELVES.

Cicero then asks if Caesar will come to the Capitol tomorrow. Casca replies that he plans to do so, and Cicero leaves.

As the dreadful storm rages on, Cassius arrives and recognizes Casca by his voice. He scolds Casca for being so afraid and argues cleverly that the storm is a warning of Rome's condition and of the evil fate it is likely to meet soon if the wrong man comes to power. When Casca takes this to be an allusion to Caesar, Cassius says simply, "Let it be who it is," adding that the Romans no longer have their ancestors' masculine fighting spirit but instead have become "womanish" in their passive submission to tyranny.

Casca observes that the Senate will reportedly offer Caesar a crown the next day, which he will be entitled to wear in all the lands Rome has conquered, except in Italy. If that happens, Cassius replies, he will use his own dagger to free himself from bondage by killing himself. Casca concurs with this sentiment. Cassius says that Caesar has one excuse for being such a tyrant: By acting like sheep, the Romans have made him act like a wolf. But Cassius wonders if he has said too much: Maybe Casca is willing to be a slave of Caesar and will report Cassius for expressing these seditious sentiments—in which case Cassius can still kill himself.

But again Casca heartily agrees with Cassius. The two men shake hands; Casca has thus joined the conspiracy to kill Caesar.

Now they are joined by another conspirator, Cinna. He is glad to learn that Casca has entered the plot. Remarking on the "strange sights" seen tonight, he hopes that Brutus can be persuaded to join "our party." Cassius reassures him, instructing him to carry the forged messages for Brutus. As Cinna departs, Cassius tells Casca that all that remains is to visit Brutus at his home and conclude the plan. From the conspirators' point of view, everything seems to be going according to plan.

ANALYSIS

Supernatural wonders break into a play that is largely notable for their absence. Astounding omens of imminent crisis abound, in defiance of human reason.

Cicero is skeptical about the meaning of all these signs, but Cassius manages to take advantage of them, convincing Casca after Cicero has left that they favor the plot against Caesar. He easily brings Casca into his scheme. When they encounter Cinna, he too seems ready to do his part to prevent Caesar from gaining the crown.

All that remains is for the plotters to clinch the noble Brutus, the most respected man in Rome, as their figurehead. And Cassius has already begun his seduction.

ACT II, SCENE 1

OVERVIEW

This turbulent night finds Brutus awake in his garden, brooding over whether the assassination of Caesar is justified. So far Caesar has actually done nothing concrete to warrant shedding his blood, but power may change his nature, making him a tyrant.

Brutus's servant boy, Lucius, brings him a letter that was thrown through the window. He asks Lucius to ascertain whether the next day is the Ides of March. (Shakespeare has abbreviated the entire month after Lupercal for dramatic effect.)

Brutus reads the letter. It is the familiar message: Shall Rome be ruled

LET'S CARVE HIM AS A DISH FIT FOR THE GODS,

by a single man? It reminds him that his great ancestor Brutus drove the tyrannical Tarquin family out of the city centuries earlier.

As Brutus reflects further, Lucius tells him that Cassius and others have come to see him. Brutus knows that the conspirators are ready to act and that the time has come. He can no longer put off his fateful decision.

These men, as Lucius notes, have hidden their faces. Brutus dislikes their furtive ways, which imply shame at what they are doing. He reasons that if they are saving Rome from tyranny, they should be proud of themselves. Their cause is Roman liberty, is it not? Then why should they behave as if they were guilty criminals?

They enter. After expressing regret for troubling Brutus at this early hour, Cassius introduces him to the other conspirators: Trebonius, Decius Brutus, Casca, Cinna, and Metellus Cimber. Cassius proposes that they take an oath together, but Brutus argues strongly against this idea. Why should a good Roman take an oath? His sincere promise should be enough. Brutus's argument prevails.

Cassius asks whether Cicero should be invited to join the plot. The others applaud this proposal, because Cicero's age and gravity will counter any assumption that the plotters are merely ruled by the hot blood of angry youth. But once again Brutus objects: Cicero, he says, will never join an enterprise begun by other men. Yet again the others change their minds and defer to Brutus.

Now Cassius raises what will prove to be the most critical point of all: Is it prudent to kill Caesar alone? He urges that Mark Antony be slain, too, for he is a dangerous enemy, a "shrewd contriver," loyal to Caesar and sure to make trouble for the assassins.

Brutus vehemently overrules Cassius. Killing Antony in addition to Caesar would be "too bloody," he argues: "Let's be sacrificers, but not butchers." Caesar's death will make Antony harmless, like the severed limb of a corpse. The plotters must seem like "purgers, not murderers." Cassius tries to object, but Brutus cuts him short. As usual, the others go along with Brutus.

The clock strikes three. Here Shakespeare commits a famous anachronism, as perfectionists love to point out: The clock did not exist in ancient Rome. But this is no blunder; the Bard would have known very well that he was taking a minor liberty with historical fact for dramatic purposes, as he did often. The sound of the clock tolling is a highly effective way of telling us how much time has passed and intensifying suspense. The hours of Caesar's life are ticking away.

"NOT HEW HIM AS A CARCASS FIT FOR HOUNDS."

Morning is imminent, and the fateful day has arrived. But will Caesar come to the Capitol? Cassius fears that Caesar has become too superstitious lately and, after listening to his augurers (fortune-tellers) interpret the fearful omens, will stay at home.

Decius, however, allays this worry. He knows how to manipulate

GREER GARSON, LEFT, PLAYED CALPURNIA, AND DEBORAH KERR PLAYED PORTIA IN HOLLYWOOD'S 1953 TREATMENT OF JULIUS CAESAR.

Caesar with flattery, no matter what the augurers may say. Now everyone is ready. The conspirators will go to Caesar's house together and escort him to the Capitol at eight o'clock.

As the others leave Brutus alone, his devoted wife, Portia, comes to him. He has been behaving strangely and irritably; she knows something is very wrong. She asks what it is. He answers evasively that his health has been bad. She rejects this answer; she knows him too well to accept it. Kneeling she begs him to tell her the truth. In order to prove her devotion to Brutus, she has given herself a gash on the thigh.

Deeply moved Brutus tells her not to kneel; he knows that he is unworthy of so noble a wife. But instead of telling her the truth, he promises to explain everything later. As someone knocks at the door, he tells her to leave him.

The new visitor is Caius Ligarius. Brutus tells him to come along to the house of the man to whom something must be done. He will explain on the way.

ANALYSIS

Cassius is called Brutus's "brother"; actually, he is Brutus's brother-in-law, married to Brutus's sister—a relation Shakespeare plays down for his purposes. He turns the actual Brutus of history, whom he found in Plutarch's *Lives* and other sources, into a much purer, more abstract character. (Three ancient historians repeated the rumor that the real Brutus was Caesar's illegitimate son; there is no hint of this in the play.)

Brutus's dislike of secrecy will have disastrous results for his party. Because he is philosophical himself, he expects other men to behave like impartial philosophers. This unrealistic temperament makes him completely unfit for politics in the real world of human passions. He will meet his nemesis in Antony, who instinctively knows everything that Brutus can never understand.

In the matter of taking oaths, admitting Cicero to the conspiracy, and assassinating Antony along with Caesar, Cassius, against his better judgment, lets Brutus have his way. Brutus wins their clashes of wills through force of character. Nobody can stand up to him.

Cassius is concerned that Caesar will heed the warnings of the augurers and stay at home. In the past people have used many methods to foretell the future, as we still do today. Most of these methods can be considered unscientific, even superstitious, such as astrology. The ancient Roman augurers often based their predictions on examination of the internal organs of birds and beasts, as is done in this play.

Shakespeare's portrayal of Portia, Brutus's wife, is fairly faithful to the ancient sources. She was in fact the daughter of the philosopher Cato, as she says in the play. And it does seem that she tried to dissuade her husband from joining the party of Caesar's enemies.

ACT II, SCENE 2

OVERVIEW

Like Brutus, Caesar is awake as the storm continues to rage. Calpurnia has had nightmares and cried out in her sleep, "Help ho! They murder Caesar!" He sends orders for the augurers to make sacrifices to determine what is about to happen.

Calpurnia enters, insisting that Caesar stay at home today. He says just as firmly that he will go to the Capitol. The things that threatened him, he says, looked only on his back; they will flee his face.

But this answer fails to satisfy Calpurnia. She names several bad omens that have been witnessed lately: a lioness giving birth on a Roman street, graves opening and yielding their dead, warriors fighting in the clouds, shrieking ghosts, and so forth. Caesar's answer is that these are warnings to the world at large, not to him in particular. He will go forth as planned. And when she adds that portents attend the deaths of princes, not beggars, he makes his famous answer:

> COWARDS DIE MANY TIMES BEFORE THEIR DEATHS;
> THE VALIANT NEVER TASTE OF DEATH BUT ONCE.

Yet as a servant enters, Caesar immediately demands to know what the augurers are saying. He is not quite as indifferent to prophecy as he pretends.

The servant informs him that the latest omen is bad: The priests have cut open an animal and found no heart in it. When Caesar dismisses this omen, too, Calpurnia begs him to stay home, letting Mark Antony tell the Senate that he is ill. This time he agrees.

At this moment Decius arrives and Caesar, scorning false excuses, instructs him simply to tell the senators that he chooses not to appear. Decius asks for a specific reason he can offer so that he will not be laughed at. Caesar maintains that he owes nobody a public reason, but for Decius's private satisfaction he explains that Calpurnia has had a nightmare of his statue spouting blood. The quick-witted conspirator comes up with a less frightening explanation of this vision, and Caesar finds it satisfying.

Besides, Decius adds cleverly, the Senate plans to offer Caesar a crown today. If it gets wind of the real reason for his refusal to appear, it will joke:

> "BREAK UP THE SENATE TILL ANOTHER TIME,
> WHEN CAESAR'S WIFE SHALL MEET
> WITH BETTER DREAMS."

What is more, it will seem that mighty Caesar is afraid. So Caesar resolves to go to the Senate after all. Just then Brutus and the other conspirators arrive; so does Antony. Everyone is now ready to go.

"WHEN BEGGARS DIE, THERE ARE NO COMETS SEEN"

ANALYSIS

Much of the suspense arises from our doubt that Caesar will show up. He has to—but will he? He hesitates, as his wife tries to prevent him from going and his enemies, playing on his vanity, try to trick him. The question of whether he will die is no question at all; but the suspense lies in seeing how the issue will be settled. We have to admire the cunning arguments of his foes, and their wit.

This scene contains much irony and humor. Caesar wants to appear firm and decisive, but he vacillates comically as Calpurnia, the augurers, and the conspirators take turns manipulating him. The most powerful man in Rome is far from what he seems to be.

ACT II, SCENE 3

OVERVIEW

Artemidorus, a writer and public speaker who loves Caesar, reads a message he has prepared for Caesar. It names the conspirators and warns him to beware of them today. If Caesar reads it, it may save his life; if he doesn't, he will probably die.

ANALYSIS

This brief scene underscores the danger Caesar faces and heightens the tension of his impending fate. We know he is about to die, yet there is still the tantalizing possibility that he will escape his almost certain doom.

ACT II, SCENE 4

Portia, with the servant boy Lucius, desperately wants to know how Brutus is. In agitation and confusion, she tells Lucius to run ahead to the Senate house and check up on him. She chances to meet the Soothsayer, who hopes to see Caesar in time to save him. She is certain what her husband is up to.

ANALYSIS

The drama continues to heighten; Caesar's peril keeps increasing. Like Artemidorus, the Soothsayer hopes to reach Caesar in time to save him.

Our own feelings are divided. We understand Brutus's belief that Caesar himself is dangerous, yet we also fear for his life, though of course we know he is about to die.

ACT III, SCENE 1

OVERVIEW

We are only midway through the play. In a tragedy the title character usually dies at the end. This time he dies startlingly early, in only the third scene in which he appears. Shakespeare's first audience must have been astounded and baffled, like the first audience for Alfred Hitchcock's film *Psycho* (1960) when the main character was killed off less than halfway through the film. How can a story recover from such a shock to the expectations?

Caesar, accompanied by his friends and enemies, taunts the Soothsayer: "The Ides of March are come." The man retorts: "Ay, Caesar, but not gone." Artemidorus implores Caesar to read his letter, but the quick Decius, sensing his purpose, urges Caesar to consider another

A NINETEENTH-CENTURY WOOD ENGRAVING DEPICTS ARTEMIDORUS IMPLORING CAESAR TO READ HIS LETTER OF WARNING.

man's plea first. When Artemidorus says that his letter is more urgent to Caesar, Caesar says he will put his own interest last. When Artemidorus persists, Caesar thinks he is insane and Publius (who is not one of the conspirators) orders him out of the way.

By hinting that he knows about the conspiracy, a new character, Popilius Lena, raises the level of suspense. In the confusion of the moment, the conspirators fear they have been found out. They must strike quickly. It is now or never.

Decius, with his usual presence of mind, calls on Metellus Cimber to present his petition to Caesar. Cimber, kneeling, does so. Caesar expresses disgust at this excessively humble behavior. Brutus and Cassius kneel, too, pretending to join Cimber's plea for his banished brother. Caesar is startled by these gestures, but he insists that nothing can change his mind, for he is "constant as the Northern star." When Cinna and Decius kneel too, he tells them not to bother, for even Brutus kneels to him in vain.

Casca stabs first. All the conspirators follow, Brutus last of all. When Caesar sees Brutus stab, he cries, "*Et tu, Brute?*" (Even you, Brutus?) and falls dead. (Many readers assume that the famous words "*Et tu, Brute?*" were the actual dying cry of the historical Caesar, but in fact Shakespeare seems to have invented them.)

After a stunned moment, the conspirators rejoice. It is a great moment for Roman liberty, they think, which will be remembered and celebrated forever. They imagine it being reenacted in plays on the stage centuries hence, in foreign languages that do not even exist yet, and themselves honored as liberators of their country. They joyfully smear themselves and their swords in Caesar's blood. Even the gentle Brutus joins in this hideous rejoicing.

Everyone except the killers leaves the scene. Suddenly a simple

PERFORMING AT THE ROYAL SHAKESPEARE THEATER IN 2006, ACTOR JAMES HAYES, IN THE FOREGROUND, PLAYS CAESAR SLAIN IN ACT III, SCENE 1.

question occurs to the ever-practical Cassius: "Where is Antony?" He already senses that the assassination has only begun a period of chaos.

Antony has "fled to his house amazed." But the killers are drunk with triumph and hardly notice.

Antony's servant arrives and falls to his knees before Brutus. He says that Antony will love Brutus and cooperate with him if only Brutus can explain why Caesar deserved to die.

Suspecting nothing, Brutus is pleased and reassured to hear this. He remarks that Antony will prove a good friend to the conspirators. Cassius is not so sure.

Antony himself arrives. He is shocked at the sight of Caesar's body, saying, "O mighty Caesar! Dost thou lie so low?" He tells Brutus and the others that if they bear him ill will, too, they should kill him at this moment; he will be happy to die now, beside Caesar.

Brutus, apologetic, tells Antony not to ask for death. Of course, he admits, the assassins must seem cruel right now, but they acted out of pity for Rome and without malice toward Caesar. Besides, Cassius adds, Antony himself will share power in the new order. (Cassius assumes that power is Antony's chief motive.) Brutus pleads with him for patience until he calms the people down by explaining why Caesar had to die.

Antony shakes the bloody hands of the conspirators, beginning with Brutus. Then he resumes speaking to Caesar's corpse, with mingled grief and rage.

Cassius interrupts him to ask whether he means to be a friend to the conspirators. Antony protests that he will be their friend, provided that they give him reasons why Caesar was dangerous. Brutus agrees, and when Antony asks to speak as Caesar's friend at the funeral, he agrees again.

This is too much for Cassius. He thinks Brutus is a fool for wanting to let Antony address the plebeians at such an occasion. What if his words inflame the people against the killers?

Brutus tells Cassius not to worry (his usual obtuse advice). He has an incurable habit of assuming that nothing can go wrong with his plans, though something always does. Here he assures Cassius that he will speak first, explaining why Caesar's death was necessary, and will tell the crowd that Antony speaks by permission, giving Caesar a proper funeral. Cassius grudgingly gives in.

Brutus tells Antony that he must not speak ill of the conspirators but must praise Caesar and acknowledge that Brutus's party is allowing him to speak. Antony readily agrees to these terms.

Left alone with the body, Antony bares his real feelings. He denounces "these butchers" and predicts a ferocious civil war throughout Italy as Caesar's enraged spirit demands revenge.

The servant of Caesar's nephew, Octavius Caesar, arrives and is overcome with grief when he sees the body. He and Antony weep together. Young Octavius, who is half as old as Antony, is still about twenty miles from Rome, and Antony tells the servant to let him know that the city is still too dangerous for him to approach. It will be wiser for him to wait to return until Antony has tested public reaction in his speech.

ANALYSIS

In this audacious scene the four chief characters fully reveal themselves. Caesar, the title character, is daringly and shockingly killed midway through the story. We see his colossal ego and self-delusion exposed; he likens himself to the fixed North Star only seconds before his death.

Shakespeare takes interesting liberties with his historical sources that make Brutus's character seem more lofty and impersonal than it really was. Not only does he suppress any hint that Brutus was actually Caesar's natural son, but he eliminates Plutarch's assertion that he put a

MARK ANTONY (TOM MANNION) MOURNS THE FALLEN CAESAR (IAN HOGG) IN A 2001 ROYAL SHAKESPEARE COMPANY PRODUCTION.

gruesome finishing touch on the slaughter by savagely stabbing Caesar in his private parts.

Brutus and Cassius achieve their purpose in the assassination, in the narrow sense of killing Caesar, but of course they utterly fail to secure liberty for Rome. In fact they achieve the opposite result: They inaugurate a period of vicious civil war, which will end with the destruction of the old constitutional republic they hoped to save—and with the tyranny and one-man rule of the empire.

Brutus assumes control of the conspiracy and blunders disastrously at every turn. Cassius's judgment is better, but he is too weak to stand up to Brutus. It is almost comical. Brutus has a perverse genius for making every bad situation worse.

The unscrupulous Antony, who cares little for Rome's traditional liberties, at least knows what he is doing and has a sure sense of how to handle men. He has none of Brutus's sentimental faith in human reason. He understands that men are ruled by their irrational passions, and that is fine by him. He never expects men to be much better than beasts.

Unlike Brutus, Cassius appreciates Antony's demagogic skill and sizes him up as a powerful adversary. But Brutus ignores his warnings and allows Antony to take the upper hand. We are about to see the consequences of Brutus's folly.

ACT III, SCENE 2

OVERVIEW

The plebeians are uneasy. Their great favorite, Caesar, has been killed, and they demand to know why. Brutus promises them a full explanation. As he steps up to the pulpit to make his speech, another group of plebeians follows Cassius, who will also make the case for Caesar's death.

Brutus begins. His speech is short and formal, using carefully balanced sentences. He insists, truly enough, that he loved Caesar, but argues that Caesar was a threat to Roman liberty. He sums up his whole argument in a single line: "Not that I loved Caesar less, but that I loved Rome more." He says he will be willing to die, too, if the good of Rome should ever require his death. His complete sincerity is obvious.

The crowd cheers. Brutus has quickly persuaded them that Caesar was a tyrant. Their fickleness is typified by their irrational enthusiasm for Brutus: "Let him be Caesar!" one member of the audience cries.

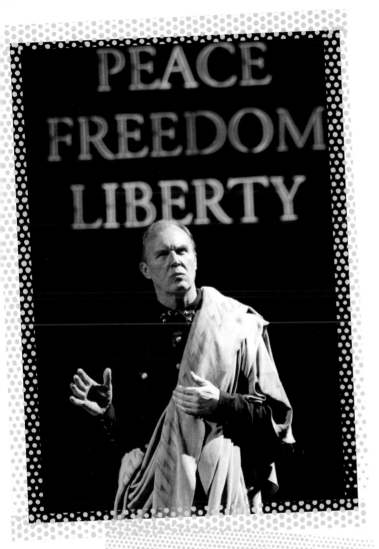

Antony arrives with Caesar's corpse, which is covered with a bloody mantle, or cloak. Brutus, departing, tells the people to stay and hear what Antony has to say. Some of them grumble that he had better speak no ill of Brutus.

Antony begins, "Friends, Romans, countrymen, lend me your ears!" He says at once that he has not come to celebrate Caesar, but to "bury" him and let the harm he has done outlive him, as it does with most men. This is not what the crowd has expected to hear from Antony, Caesar's close friend. He seems to be going further than Brutus in depreciating the dead man. What is going on?

Antony stresses that he is speaking with the permission of Brutus and the others, all of whom are "honorable" men. Yes, Caesar was his friend, "faithful and just" to him. But Brutus says he was ambitious, and after all, Brutus is honorable. True, Caesar brought captives to Rome, greatly enriching the city with their ransoms. Maybe this showed his ambition, too? And it is true that he wept for the Roman poor. This may not have seemed ambitious of him, but Brutus does accuse him of ambition, and Brutus is too honorable to lie.

Already Antony's repetition of the word *honorable* is starting to sound a shade sarcastic, and now Antony repeats it again, even more boldly: You all, he reminds the crowd, saw me offer Caesar the crown three times on the feast of Lupercal, and you saw him refuse it all three times! "Was this ambition?" Now his irony is unmistakable and undisguised:

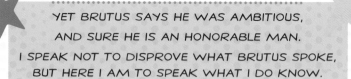

YET BRUTUS SAYS HE WAS AMBITIOUS,
AND SURE HE IS AN HONORABLE MAN.
I SPEAK NOT TO DISPROVE WHAT BRUTUS SPOKE,
BUT HERE I AM TO SPEAK WHAT I DO KNOW.

He is already, only a few sentences into his speech, virtually calling Brutus a liar. He accuses the crowd of fickleness: Have they forgotten their love for Caesar so soon? Making a pun with Brutus's name, he likens the people to "brutish beasts" that have lost their powers of reason. He

"I COME TO BURY CAESAR, NOT TO PRAISE HIM."

pauses to let his words take effect. (In truth, he is taking quick, aggressive advantage of their mutable emotions, not their reason.)

The plebeians begin to mutter that Caesar has been wronged. Very soon they start swaying to Antony. One person remarks, "There's not a nobler man in Rome than Antony."

Now Antony cuts loose, savagely roasting Brutus and Cassius, these "honorable men." There is no doubt about what he means. After only a couple of minutes, he has completely turned the tables on his enemies. The crowd is his. He holds up a parchment, which he identifies as Caesar's will. He says he will not read it, because it would have so powerful an impact on the people if they heard what Caesar has left to them.

Of course this drives the crowd wild. They insist on hearing the will immediately.

But Antony, master of manipulation, tells them to be patient, saying, "I must not read it." Being made of flesh and blood, not wood or stone, they would erupt in fury if they knew its contents. (Antony makes multiple appeals, first to their sentimental love for Caesar and indignation at his killing, then to their curiosity and greed.)

Antony, by mentioning the will at all, professes to regret wronging "the honorable men/Whose daggers have stabbed Caesar." The crowd screams that they were traitors, villains, and murderers, and demands to hear the will.

Antony comes down from the pulpit and tells the people to make a ring around Caesar's corpse, so that he may show them the man who wrote the will. He brings their passions, already violent, to an even higher pitch.

"If you have tears," he says, slightly lowering the emotional level, "prepare to shed them now." He points to the bloody cloak over the dead body, recalling the first time Caesar ever wore it, on the day of his great victory over the Nervii. (Actually, Antony was not present that day; he joined Caesar's army three years later. But neither the plebeians nor we the reader care about that; we are all swept up in the momentum of his speech.) He points out the holes made by the conspirators' stabs—Casca first, then Cassius, and finally Brutus. (Again, everyone forgets that Antony was actually absent during the assassination. Who cares?)

With his matchless sense of drama, Antony points to the bloodiest hole as the one left by Brutus—"the most unkindest cut of all," the one that broke Caesar's heart and finally killed him. (Both Antony and Shakespeare know just how to handle an audience.) *This* was the triumph of "bloody treason."

Antony asks the people why they weep at the mere sight of Caesar's gory clothing. Pulling the cloak off, he bids them to behold the body itself.

The effect is potent: They scream for revenge—"Let not a traitor live!"

Antony now adopts a modest tone. He asks the crowd not to let him stir them to mutiny and rage against those "honorable" men, the assassins. He professes not to be an orator like Brutus, but only "a plain blunt man/ That love my friend"; he claims he is merely pouring out his feelings. But if their roles were reversed, a Brutus in Antony's place would drive the city

THIS WAS THE MOST UNKINDEST CUT OF ALL

mad with the power of his eloquence. The stones of Rome themselves would come alive in fury!

As the plebeians keep calling for the conspirators' deaths—only minutes after cursing Caesar and cheering Brutus—Antony teases them for forgetting the will he spoke of. Again they call on him to read it to them.

He tells them that Caesar has left every Roman citizen seventy-five drachmas (ancient silver coins), as well as all his parks and gardens for them to enjoy walking in. They cheer and riot, vowing death to the "traitors."

As the plebeians riot, Antony says to himself in satisfaction:

> MISCHIEF, THOU ART AFOOT:
> TAKE THOU WHAT COURSE THOU WILT.

A servant brings Antony word that Octavius has already come to Rome. Meanwhile Brutus and Cassius, fleeing for their lives, have left the city.

ANALYSIS

Brutus, seeking to calm the plebeians, really thinks he can win them over with an honest appeal to their reason and love of the common good. If only he can prove to them that Rome's welfare required Caesar to die, he is sure that they will be satisfied. Unlike Cassius and Antony, he has no idea of the motives that really move men, such as loyalty and greed. Above all he is blind to the speed with which people's emotions can change.

Brutus's speech is a polished piece of rhetoric, in carefully balanced parallel sentences. It sounds perfectly reasonable, and the crowd accepts his argument and applauds him, but the plebeians are only superficially moved. Their mild reception of his oration teaches him nothing. Antony is about to give him the lesson of his life in how to manage a crowd.

Brutus is sometimes compared to Hamlet, another intellectual hero who hesitates to kill, but we can hardly imagine Hamlet being so naive about human nature. Brutus really thinks he can sway the emotional mob by appealing to its better nature with fine rhetoric, as if he were addressing a crowd of impartial philosophers. The street-smart Antony knows better. He realizes the obvious: that Rome is ready to explode. He sees his chance to turn the tables on Caesar's assassins and he makes the most of it.

Using bitter sarcasm and savage irony about his enemies, Antony shrewdly appeals to the crowd's passions, such as fury and greed. Step

RALPH FIENNES PLAYED MARK ANTONY AT THE BARBICAN, LONDON, IN 2005.

by step, with a perfect sense of what to say next with each sentence and each carefully chosen word, Antony rips away at Brutus's sincerest appeals as if they were bald lies. He makes the word *honorable*, the very word Brutus lives by, a cruel joke. He mercilessly mocks Brutus's earnest claim that he loved Caesar, making him sound utterly treacherous to his truest friend.

At the same time Antony knows how to confuse his listeners by changing the subject. In the midst of their moral outrage at the murder, he introduces the separate topic of Caesar's will and what it provides for each of them. And he uses this new subject to build suspense. In fact he makes up the terms of the will to tickle the crowd's mercenary fancies; they are empty promises.

Truly Antony knows every trick in the book. Through him Shakespeare displays a vast knowledge of classical rhetorical figures, with such intimidating Greek names as *anaphora*, *epistrophe*, *epizeuxis*, *exclamatio*, *exuscitatio*, *isocolon*, *oxymoron*, *parison*, *prosopopeia*, and *synoeciosis*, to mention only a few that scholars have identified. Antony never employs such fifty-dollar words. On the contrary he uses simple language that always seems natural, heartfelt, and spontaneous. Nobody suspects him of being anything but what he says he is: "a plain blunt man/That love my friend."

It is all a horrible distortion of the reality, but the ruthless Antony has the skilled orator's art of making it seem totally plausible. He proves himself diabolically brilliant.

Nor is Antony, in contrast to the scrupulous Brutus, above lying and falsifying the facts for dramatic effect. He recalls the first time Caesar wore the mantle he died in, the day he defeated the Nervii. But in fact, this triumph occurred years before Antony joined Caesar's army. Another falsehood is more obvious: Antony specifies the hole that each of the killers made in the cloak. How easily we forget that Antony had left the Senate *before* the death of Caesar and could not have witnessed what he now pretends to remember in such minute and graphic detail!

When he has finished, the conspirators have to run for their lives. Cassius's misgivings about giving Antony equal time are more than fully vindicated. His own passions have made him prophetic. Why did he let Brutus overrule his misgivings?

The crowd is almost a separate character. Though fickle they are basically prosperous and contented (unlike, say, the starving plebeians of Shakespeare's *Coriolanus*). One minute they are cheering Brutus, while only moments later they are cheering Antony and screaming for Brutus's blood.

Many have taken Shakespeare's depiction of the Roman mob as evidence that he opposed democracy. There may be some truth in this, but it might be more accurate to say that his skepticism about the mob merely reflects his view of human nature as fluid, arbitrary, and unpredictable, in both the individual and the mass.

ACT III, SCENE 3

OVERVIEW

Cinna, a poet, is walking alone in the street, thinking of a strange dream he had of feasting with Caesar. Something tells him he should stay at home, but he feels himself mysteriously drawn forth.

He meets a group of angry plebeians who demand to know his name and where he is going. He tries to answer reasonably, if a bit humorously, but they are in no mood for either reason or humor.

When they learn that his name is Cinna, they mistake him for Cinna the conspirator. He assures them he is Cinna the poet, but this fails to assuage them in their bloodthirsty temper. "Tear him for his bad verses!"

one member of this mob cries. He keeps protesting that he is not Cinna the conspirator, but they kill him anyway.

As Antony has said, mischief is afoot. He has whipped the plebeians into an insane frenzy, and a poet becomes their first victim. As Antony has also put it, "Men have lost their reason." This is the ultimate result of his own great oration. Men have indeed turned into beasts.

Brutus's hope that Caesar's death would breed a new era of liberty has come to this.

ACT IV, SCENE 1

OVERVIEW

Many months later, Antony, young Octavius Caesar, and Lepidus, Rome's new ruling trio (or "triumvirate"), are checking a list of names of prominent Romans, arbitrarily deciding which ones shall die (without trials, of course). Lepidus readily agrees to his own brother's death, if Antony's nephew is killed, too; Antony agrees just as quickly.

Antony sends Lepidus to Caesar's house to fetch the will. They must decide how to limit the keeping of all the promises Antony has made to the plebeians.

As soon as Lepidus is gone, Antony belittles him behind his back, saying he is "a slight unmeritable man," fit to be used only for errands, like a pack animal, but absurdly unfit to be one of the three most powerful men in the mighty Roman Empire. Octavius asks, then, why Antony chose him to be one of the three new rulers. We can use him for the time being, Antony answers, but at this moment we must deal with the armies that Brutus and Cassius have raised.

"FORTUNE IS MERRY, AND IN THIS MOOD WILL GIVE US ANYTHING"

ANALYSIS

The savage killing of Cinna the poet was only our first hint of the black and lawless era into which Caesar's assassination has plunged Rome. Now we see how serious the situation really is. The new rulers are freely sentencing men to death. So much for Roman liberty! Brutus's plot has brought about an even worse tyranny than he feared from Caesar.

Among other things, Antony has to deal with Caesar's will. The triumvirate cannot afford to keep the lavish promises Antony made in his speech; he was lying about the terms of the will in order to win the crowd's favor, promising the impossible, as any demagogue would. The money he pledged—seventy-five drachmas per citizen—was part of the elaborate lie.

At least Brutus tried to tell the truth; he made no such promises to the people. He wrongly thought he was giving the people freedom, but he meant what he said in good faith. Though he was terribly naïve about human nature and politics, he was at least sincere. But this is what his honesty has led to: disaster for Rome.

ACT IV, SCENE 2

OVERVIEW

At their camp in Asia Minor, an angry Cassius comes to visit Brutus, whom he feels has seriously wronged him. Brutus rejects this charge, saying that he does not even wrong his enemies; how, then, could he wrong his brother-in-law Cassius?

At any rate he tells Cassius to refrain from accusing him in front of their armies, who should never see discord between the two leaders. Their differences can be resolved privately, in his tent.

ANALYSIS

For the first time we see open ill will between Brutus and Cassius. Until now their tensions have been subdued.

Cassius shows his hot temper, while Brutus displays his habitual calm. He also demonstrates a touch of typical self-righteousness when he says that he is incapable of wronging an enemy, let alone a brother.

But like the responsible leader he is, he prefers not to let their followers see their differences; these can be settled discreetly, out of sight.

ACT IV, SCENE 3

OVERVIEW

Inside Brutus's tent Cassius vents his rage. Brutus has disgraced him by condemning one of his men, Lucius Pella, for accepting bribes and ignoring Cassius's letters pleading for him. Brutus answers that Cassius should never have tried to defend the culprit. When Cassius says that such small crimes should be overlooked at times like this, Brutus remarks that Cassius himself is widely known for taking bribes.

This really enrages Cassius, who swears that he would kill anyone but Brutus for making such a charge. Brutus's calm reply is that only Cassius could get away with such corruption. Ignoring Cassius's violent rage, Brutus reminds him that they killed Caesar for justice's sake and for "supporting robbers." (This is the first we have heard of this charge against Caesar; earlier, in Act II, the brooding Brutus was unable to think of any actual crime warranting Caesar's death!)

Now the fur is flying. Cassius warns Brutus to stop baiting him, the more experienced soldier. The two men exchange hot words, and Cassius all but threatens violence. Brutus refuses to be intimidated, laughing off the threat: You may terrify your slaves this way, he says, but not me!

Cassius begins to back down, though he again threatens to something he may regret; to which Brutus retorts that he has already done things he should regret.

> THERE IS NO TERROR, CASSIUS, IN YOUR THREATS;
> FOR I AM ARMED SO STRONG IN HONESTY
> THAT THEY PASS BY ME AS THE IDLE WIND,
> WHICH I RESPECT NOT.

Yet Brutus, boasting of his own honor, now complains that Cassius has refused to give him the money he requested—the same money he accuses Cassius of raising corruptly! Nobody in this story is quite pure, not even the noble Brutus.

Cassius accuses Brutus of not loving him and pulls out his dagger, offering it to Brutus to kill him. Brutus makes fun of this melodramatic emotionalism. Cassius admits that he deserves some blame for his ill temper, and so does Brutus. In a moment they are both apologizing, warm friends again, their good humor restored.

Cassius marvels that Brutus could have been so angry. Brutus explains that he has been enduring "many griefs." Cassius urges him to bear evils like the Stoic philosopher he is. Brutus reveals that Portia is dead.

Shocked by this news, Cassius marvels that Brutus refrained from killing him during their quarrel. He asks what she died of. Brutus explains that his own absence, coupled with the threat posed by the armies of Antony and Octavius, drove her to despair and suicide. Portia's suicide is foreshadowed by her earlier unsettled, even extreme, behavior, as when she gashed her thigh to prove her "constancy." In ancient Rome, however, suicide could be a matter of honor, not just of individual psychology (depression). Both men drink wine in remembrance of this remarkable woman.

Their friends Titinius and Messala join them to discuss other news of their enemies. Not only are Antony and Octavius bringing their mighty forces to do battle at Philippi, but they are also continuing their bloody purges in Rome. A hundred senators have been put to death by proscription (that is, by mere decree, without the trials to which the law should have entitled them); among these, shockingly, is the great orator Cicero, the most eloquent philosopher in Rome.

Messala asks Brutus whether he has had letters from Portia; Brutus says he has not. Messala tells him she is dead; Brutus seems to accept this stoically. (Scholars argue over this passage; is the repetition of the news of Portia's death a deliberate touch by Shakespeare, or a mere editing error?)

Brutus and Cassius disagree over whether to take the initiative against the enemy at Phillipi. Cassius favors a passive strategy, letting the armies of Antony and Octavius wear themselves out in pursuit. Brutus thinks it is better to attack the enemy now, before the initiative and its advantages are lost; so good an opportunity may never come again. As usual Cassius yields and lets Brutus decide.

As they part company for the night, Cassius regrets their earlier quarrel and expresses his deep affection for Brutus. The men retire. Brutus sweetly asks the drowsy Lucius, his servant boy, to play a few strains of music on his lute before he falls asleep. As the boy dozes off, Brutus gently takes the instrument from him to prevent its getting broken by accident.

Intending to do a little reading before he sleeps, Brutus is surprised to see someone in his tent: the ghost of Caesar. He asks who it is. It replies,

"Thy evil spirit, Brutus." Why has it come here? "To tell thee thou shalt see me at Philippi," it says. Then it vanishes.

Brutus shouts, awakening all the other people in the tent. He asks them whether they have seen anything. They have not. Caesar's ghost has appeared to Brutus alone.

ANALYSIS

This eventful scene opens with the first open breach between Brutus and Cassius. We learn of Cassius's dishonesty, but also of Brutus's own

A HAND-COLORED LITHOGRAPH (CIRCA 1880) DEPICTS CAESAR'S GHOST APPEARING TO BRUTUS.

corruption. Brutus also exposes an unpleasant moral smugness that for a while lowers our esteem for him. But after a bruising exchange of words verging on violence, the two are reconciled, and we learn that Portia is dead by suicide. Unknown to Cassius (and the audience), Brutus has been quietly carrying a heavy emotional burden.

This only deepens the two men's mutual love. We forgive them both for any faults we have discovered in them. As the long evening draws to a close (Shakespeare has a way of making a single busy scene seem to cover a great span of time; compare the first scene of *Hamlet*), Brutus, alone with his servant boy Lucius, shows a movingly tender side of himself. By the time he sees Caesar's ghost we feel we have gotten to know him more intimately than ever.

ACT V, SCENE 1

OVERVIEW

Antony, Octavius, and their army prepare to meet the enemy forces at Philippi in northern Greece. Octavius reminds Antony that he had predicted that the enemy would avoid such a direct attack as they now face. Antony replies that this is a mere bluff. As a messenger brings news that the enemy approaches, the two men begin to differ, as Brutus and Cassius did earlier but without anger. Not wishing to quarrel with the older Antony, Octavius asserts his authority like a monarch.

They hold a meeting with Brutus and Cassius. Sardonic and furious words are exchanged, with Antony and Octavius accusing the conspirators of cowardice, hypocrisy, and treachery for fawning on Caesar before stabbing him. Cassius tells Brutus that these insults are the bitter reward they get for allowing Antony to live instead of killing him with Caesar. Cassius also taunts Octavius as a "schoolboy" and Antony as a playboy— "a masker and a reveler."

The two armies part to prepare for the final, fateful battle. Cassius and Brutus get ready for the worst. Cassius recalls that this is his birthday, and he has changed his mind: Until now he has shared the view of the philosopher Epicurus that the gods are indifferent to men's fortunes, but he has partly come to believe in divine omens, especially the bad omens that the conspirators have seen.

Cassius tells Brutus that this may be their last chance to speak to one another; he asks Brutus what he intends to do. Brutus says he disdains suicide, believing that a man should endure whatever fate the gods choose for him.

Then, asks Cassius, you would be content to be taken back to Rome as a prisoner, and led through the streets in triumph? No, Brutus says emphatically, but since this may indeed be their final meeting forever, he proposes that they make a good farewell now.

ANALYSIS

The enemies meet for the last time before their final battle. Their mutual contempt is unaltered. There is no mystery about the likely outcome. Brutus and Cassius realize that this is their last stand and that they must brace themselves for total defeat. They discuss how best to face the end. Cassius's old Epicurean disdain for the gods and their warnings has softened, while Brutus's stern philosophical disapproval of suicide also seems to be changing as he imagines being taken back to Rome as a prisoner. We are moved as we see events having an impact on these two strong men who imagined that they could control events.

ACT V, SCENE 2

OVERVIEW

Brutus orders Messala to attack Octavius's army at once. The enemy soldiers, he says, are dispirited, and a sudden offensive should defeat them.

The excitement of the battle is conveyed by Brutus's enthusiasm. He still thinks victory is possible. As always he is too optimistic.

ACT V, SCENE 3

OVERVIEW

The events of this scene are clearer in performance than on the page, where they are apt to confuse the reader. They confuse Cassius himself, whose suicide is partly the result of misunderstanding. (It is a good idea to read the scene, slowly, at least twice!)

Cassius cries out to his friend Titinius (whom he had briefly mentioned to Brutus in Act I) that his own men are retreating; he has killed one of these cowards himself. Titinius tells him that Brutus "gave the word too early," causing the soldiers to begin looting while they were surrounded by Antony's men. (Shakespeare is much less clear than usual here. Plutarch, his source for the details of the battle, is partly to blame. There are simply too many characters to keep track of; some of them appear here for the first time in the play. Battle scenes are always tricky to write understandably.)

Pindarus arrives and urges Cassius to retreat further; Antony's men are in Cassius's tents. Cassius, whose eyesight is poor, sees tents aflame and asks Titinius, "Are those my tents where I perceive the fire?" When Titinius assures him that they are, Cassius orders him to ride and find out whether the attackers are friend or enemy. He also orders Pindarus to go up a nearby hill and report what he can see.

Cassius again mentions that this is his birthday; his life has come full circle, to end on the anniversary of its beginning. He calls out to Pindarus, who calls back that Titinus is surrounded by horsemen—then that he has been captured. As Antony's men shout for joy, Cassius orders Pindarus to come back and calls himself a coward for living so long as to see his best friend captured. Pindarus returns.

Cassius orders Pindarus, a servant whom he once took as a prisoner in Parthia, to kill him. He dies on his own sword, the same one with which he stabbed Caesar. Pindarus resolves to flee this country and live somewhere else, where the Romans will never find him.

Now Titinius comes back; Messala is with him. Messala tells Titinius that Brutus's men have defeated Octavius, just as Antony's men have defeated Cassius's. Titinius remarks that this news should comfort Cassius.

The two men see Cassius's body. Titinius says this means the end of the old Rome they have known. He adds that Cassius killed himself because he thought Titinius had been captured. Messala observes that melancholy, or (in modern terms) depression, often causes men to make such errors.

Messala tells Titinius to find Pindarus, while he himself takes the bad news of Cassius's death to Brutus. When Messala is gone, Titinius speaks to the corpse, asking Cassius how he could have made such a mistake. He realizes that Cassius has misconstrued everything, including the soldiers' happy shouts. He takes up Cassius's sword and kills himself.

Messala returns with Brutus and young Cato. When they find Titinius's body with Cassius's, Brutus blames their deaths on Caesar's spirit: "O Julius Caesar, thou art mighty yet." He mourns Cassius as "the last of all the Romans" and promises to mourn him properly later. For now there is a battle to finish.

ANALYSIS

In this long and tangled scene, Shakespeare renders the chaos of war and battle. Cassius, afflicted with poor eyesight to begin with, is unable to make sense of what he sees and hears. Thinking his best friend Titinius has been captured by the enemy, he kills himself. This in turn causes Titinius to commit suicide as well. And Brutus, seeing their bodies together, concludes that the spirit of Julius Caesar has brought all this on. Of course Brutus has no way of knowing that this is just what Antony prophesied in his soliloquy only a few minutes after Caesar's death.

ACT V, SCENE 4

OVERVIEW

Accompanied by Messala, Lucilius, Flavius (not the tribune Flavius of the play's opening scene), and young Cato, Brutus urges his men to keep fighting; then he leaves with Messala and Flavius.

A BATTLE SCENE FROM MGM'S 1953 FILM, DIRECTED BY JOSEPH L. MANKIEWICZ.

Young Cato boasts that he is the son of Marcus Cato. Enemy soldiers arrive, and he dies in combat. Lucilius likewise boasts that he is Brutus; enemy soldiers believe him and he is captured.

Antony comes upon them and they proudly tell him that they have caught Brutus. Of course Antony, who has been acquainted with Brutus, immediately knows better. Lucilius assures him that the real Brutus is safe and will never let himself be taken alive. Antony explains to the soldiers that they have the wrong man, but he expresses his admiration for the brave Lucilius and orders that he be accorded the kindest treatment. He would rather have such a valiant man for a friend than an enemy.

ANALYSIS

We see the valor of Brutus's men. Not only are they prepared to fight to the death, but they are also willing to be mistaken for Brutus. Such is the level of honor and nobility among the Romans. Antony recognizes and salutes it. As part of the dominance of action over words in this act, the audience needs to see some fighting and killing, and the death of young Cato is an additional sign on the theater stage that Brutus's army is being whittled away.

ACT V, SCENE 5

Brutus asks his friends and servants Clitus, Dardanus, and Volumnius to kill him. All three refuse to do so.

To Volumnius he remarks that although the enemy has won, it is more honorable to die voluntarily than to await death at the enemy's hands. Finally he bids the three farewell and rejoices: Not only have all his friends been faithful to him, but his enemies, Antony and Octavius, have won only a "vile conquest" by usurping power. Brutus will have earned more glory in his defeat than they in their victory.

At last, with his servant Strato holding his sword, Brutus runs onto it and kills himself.

As Antony, Octavius, Messala, Lucilius, and the soldiers arrive, Strato tells them that Brutus has taken his own life, thereby denying his enemies the honor of conquering him. Lucilius thanks the dead Brutus for proving him right in saying that he would never be taken alive.

Antony gives Brutus a generous eulogy, calling him "the noblest Roman of them all." The other conspirators killed Caesar maliciously; Brutus, on the other hand, joined them because of his sincere Roman patriotism.

Octavius speaks the last words of the play, agreeing with Antony's generous assessment of their great enemy. He orders an honorable burial for Brutus.

ANALYSIS

Caesar's spirit, "ranging for revenge" just as Antony foresaw and as Caesar's ghost predicted, has now claimed the lives of his killers. Violence has failed to save Roman liberty. The conspiracy has ended in tragedy.

In his salute to Brutus, Antony basically retracts everything he said against Brutus in his great funeral oration. There he was one of the "traitors"—in fact "Caesar's angel," who inflicted "the most unkindest cut of all." Now Antony in effect admits that he was lying in order to inflame the plebeians. The speech was a tremendous feat of political rhetoric, but it was as dishonest as Brutus's speech was sincere.

Octavius now assumes command as Caesar's heir by giving the orders for Brutus's funeral and the sharing of the spoils of battle. Shakespeare usually gives the final speech to the highest ranking of the surviving characters. Hail, Octavius Caesar!

LIST OF CHARACTERS

Julius Caesar (who also appears as a ghost)

Marcus Brutus, senator, leader of the conspiracy against Caesar

Caius Cassius, brother-in-law of Brutus;
another conspirator against Caesar

Mark Antony, friend of Caesar;
one of the triumvirs after his death

Octavius Caesar, nephew of Julius Caesar; another triumvir

Lepidus, the third triumvir

Casca, Trebonius, Decius Brutus, Metellus Cimber,
Cinna, Caius Ligarius: conspirators

Flavius, Marullus: tribunes of the people

Cicero, Publius, Popilius Laena: senators

Soothsayer

Artemidorus

Cinna the poet

Lucius, Brutus's servant

Pindarus, Cassius's bondsman

Titinius, an officer in Cassius's army

Lucilius, Messala, Varro, Claudius, Cato, Strato, Volumnius,
Flavius, Dardanus, Clitus: officers and soldiers in Brutus's army

Poet

Cobbler

Carpenter

Messenger

Senators, servants, plebeians, soldiers, attendants

Calpurnia, wife of Caesar

Portia, wife of Brutus

ANALYSIS OF MAJOR CHARACTERS

JULIUS CAESAR

The play of course revolves around its title figure, Julius Caesar. Whether he should be regarded as the tragic hero, however, is another question. Most of Shakespeare's tragic heroes dominate the action and die at the end of the story. Caesar acts less than he is acted upon; he appears in only

IN A 2005 PRODUCTION AT THE BARBICAN, A CORPORATE-LOOKING CAESAR (JOHN SHRAPNEL) GREETS HIS PUBLIC.

THE EVIL THAT MEN DO LIVES AFTER THEM:

three scenes, two of them rather briefly; and his ghost appears even more briefly, late in the play.

Critics have never fully agreed about Shakespeare's Caesar. Is he meant to be a great leader, a vain fool, or both? We are never really told. Shakespeare nearly always leaves some room for doubt about his major characters.

Caesar is a peerless military conqueror, whose victories all the way to what is now England have shaped Europe to this day. Western civilization and the whole world are what they are even now because of him. In that sense he remains one of the greatest and most important men who ever lived. It is hard to imagine what the world would be like today if he had never existed.

On the other hand Shakespeare has no illusions about him. Caesar has a monstrous ego. He orders the Romans to write down every word he speaks; he wants to consolidate and increase his power, no matter how much he gets; he seems to want to be king, and refuses the crown, when Antony offers it to him, only with obvious reluctance; he often refers to himself in the third person—as "Caesar," not just "I"; he makes huge boasts about his fearlessness and constancy, which are contradicted by his own words and conduct; pretending to be godlike, he is wavering and superstitious, qualities that make it easy for others to manipulate him; and he is afraid of being laughed at. His wife's nightmares frighten him, but he tries to hide this fact from the public. (He scorns the Soothsayer as a mere "dreamer.") Full of fears himself, he wants the world to fear him.

Shakespeare contrasts the public Caesar—mighty, arrogant, insolent, intimidating, and unique in history—with the weak and fallible private man. This difference is one of the prominent themes of the play. Unlike the conscientious Brutus, Caesar is never shown in a morally reflective or introspective soliloquy, concerned for the good of Rome as a whole. He is completely self-centered.

Still Caesar can be a shrewd judge of men, as he shows in the succinct way he sizes up Cassius, who shuns common pleasures such as plays and music, rarely smiles, reads a great deal, is a great observer of others, and "thinks too much." He has a sense of humor, which he shows by teasing Antony about his late-night reveling. He also shows a sense of humor in a negative way—in his fear of looking ridiculous if he lets Calpurnia's dreams deter him from appearing at the Senate. He is highly and intelligently conscious of appearances—a masterful politician.

It is a dramatic masterstroke of Shakespeare to have Caesar killed only halfway though the story, when the very name of the play leads the reader or spectator to expect that he will die in the final scene, like nearly all other tragic heroes. But the play concerns not only the individual's fate (that is not even its focus), but the rippling impact of his death on everyone and everything around him.

The destruction of the tragic hero always affects much more than the hero himself. *Julius Caesar* is unusual in studying the way Caesar's fall continues to have cascading results for both his friends and enemies.

THE GOOD IS OFT INTERRED WITH THEIR BONES.

Brutus is often taken to be the play's real tragic hero. He imagines, in a fatal error, that he can kill the spirit of Caesar by killing Caesar's body. His great intelligence is not matched by wisdom, human insight, or any fitness for political action.

Both Antony and Cassius, sharp tacticians, run circles around Brutus. Yet they both respect the nobility of his nature, as all the Romans do. Honor is everything to Brutus. This is why Cassius knows Brutus will be a priceless asset to the conspiracy against Caesar: Nobody can suspect him of acting out of selfish ambition.

Often likened to Hamlet for brooding about how he should act when faced with the supreme crisis of his life, Brutus has none of Hamlet's mercurial wit or quick, cynical perception about the people he deals with. He never makes us laugh or smile, as the witty Hamlet does. The stoical Brutus, we might almost say, is his own Horatio, enduring the trials of fortune (and misfortune) without passion or complaint.

He kills Caesar without malice, for the good of Rome. For Brutus this is an agonizing duty in which he can take no pleasure. In fact he is so obsessed with doing his duty that he never faces an obvious question: So what if Caesar has actually committed no crime yet? For the moralistic Brutus it is enough that Caesar may, like the serpent's egg, be dangerous at some time in the future. Brutus never asks whether he himself may be dangerous.

As for the actual political consequences of the assassination that all the other characters regard as vital, as far as Brutus is concerned, they hardly matter. He lacks Caesar's and Cassius's powers of observing others and judging their motives. He is completely focused on the abstract issues of right and wrong, and he is barely aware of the objective world around him. This trait makes him universally respected, widely loved, and politically calamitous.

DENZEL WASHINGTON PLAYED BRUTUS AT THE BELASCO THEATER ON BROADWAY IN 2005.

Brutus ignores his wife Portia's prophetic reservations. Like Caesar's wife, Calpurnia, she tries to warn and save her husband from some ill-defined peril. Brutus recognizes Portia's nobility—he thanks the gods for it—but he goes ahead with his fatal plan anyway. Later her suicide will remind him that she was right, but this fact is wasted on him; experience teaches him very little. (He will die still thinking that every man he has ever known has been true to him.)

After the assassination Brutus fails to see the patent danger posed by Antony, Caesar's devoted friend. He thinks he can merely appeal to Antony's reason and public spirit by arguing that Caesar was a threat to Rome and therefore had to die. Hearing this Cassius can hardly believe his own ears. How can Brutus be such a fool? He really wants to let Antony speak at the funeral! Is he mad? But Brutus is, as always, quite sincere and earnest. His only thought is to be fair to everyone, expecting fairness in return.

Brutus is just as naïve about the plebeians. He thinks it will be enough to reason with them, as if he were addressing an assembly of disinterested philosophers. What dreamworld does he imagine he is living in? Never for a moment does he suspect Antony of preparing a trap for him.

MARK ANTONY

If Brutus always seems far more attentive to his own conscience than to the world around him, Antony is extremely alert to others and their reactions. He loves partying, drinking, sports, going to plays, and, of course, politics. Fun-loving and sociable, he has a brilliant sarcastic wit. (Yet another side of him, the great lover, will come to the fore in another tragedy, *Antony and Cleopatra*. But even there he is recognizably the same dynamic and magnetic character we meet in *Julius Caesar*.)

Antony's sense of outrage is personal, not moral; when Caesar is killed, his loyalty to his friend makes him respond violently, never mind the justifications the conspirators may offer. Nobody could be more opposite to Brutus.

Antony is also unlike Brutus in his ability to disguise his real feelings. While he pretends to accept the necessity of the assassination, he instantly resolves to use Caesar's death to incite a horrible civil war. In that way he is quite ruthless; the prospect of bloodshed and slaughtered children does not disturb him. He is superbly masculine, and we cannot imagine

"O MIGHTY CAESAR! DOST THOU LIE SO LOW?"

him letting a woman touch his conscience as Portia touches Brutus's.

Cunningly Antony seems to acquiesce in Brutus's act even as they stand over Caesar's corpse, but he is consumed with an inward rage that he somehow keeps hidden. We learn of it only when he is alone. His furious soliloquy as he addresses the body as a "bleeding piece of earth" is in complete contrast to Brutus's ethical meditations. Antony is determined to make trouble, to avenge Caesar's death at any cost.

Later, when he has turned the tables on Brutus and his party, Antony will lead a cynical purge of Rome's survivors, readily agreeing to the death of his own sister's son as well as to that of such men as the great Cicero. Moral sensitivity is not among his qualities. Yet in the end, when his enemies have been destroyed, he is capable of saluting Brutus as the noblest of all Romans, the only conspirator who sincerely tried to do what was best for his country.

CASSIUS

Is Cassius the villain of *Julius Caesar*, as he is sometimes said to be? The question is not easy to answer. Of course he initiates the conspiracy to kill Caesar, he enlists Brutus in the plot, he even speaks of seducing him, and his motives are more spiteful than principled.

It has been said that a story is as good as its villain, but this is a formula for melodrama; even the worst of Shakespeare's villains are recognizably human, and complex enough to make some claim on our sympathies. The great French director Jean Renoir was once asked why his films had no villains. He explained by quoting one of his characters: "Everyone has his reasons." This was a very Shakespearean answer. Shakespeare himself puts it beautifully in a single line in *Troilus and Cressida*: "One touch of nature makes the whole world kin." In that sense Cassius, too, has his reasons. If he is a villain he is at least not a monster. His mixed qualities, some of them admirable, make him akin to all of us.

One of Cassius's outstanding traits is his keen intelligence. When Antony seems willing to cooperate with Caesar's killers, Cassius is quick to smell a rat. He knows what they are dealing with: a dangerous enemy. Yet when Brutus accepts Antony's word with no guarantees, Cassius lets Brutus overrule his better judgment, ensuring disaster.

As Caesar perceived earlier, Cassius is a shrewd judge of men. He is immune to all the common amusements that others love, such as music, games, and plays. He has a certain self-mocking humor, but he never lets it get out of control; he is not one for belly laughs or riotous mirth. Convivial he is not. Nobody would call Cassius "one of the boys."

Caesar is also quite right when he notes that men like Cassius resent anyone they see as superior to themselves; the "envious" (that is, spiteful) Cassius hates Caesar precisely because "this man is now become a god." Cassius is forced to submit to a creature no better than himself. He must have revenge on any man who holds authority over him.

Yet Cassius really respects and loves Brutus for his nobility of nature, and he is sincerely moved when he learns of Portia's death. Brutus's rebukes for his corruption—Cassius is notorious for accepting bribes—deeply wound him, yet, after threatening to kill Brutus for insulting him, he forgives this insult as he could never forgive Caesar. There is something noble in Cassius after all.

Whatever his faults Cassius is not amoral, and he dies with dignity on the same sword with which he killed the mighty Caesar. Shakespeare endows his character with a redeeming complexity. We may not esteem or trust him, but he is impossible to hate.

PORTIA

Portia is to Brutus what Horatio is to Hamlet: a touchstone. Like Horatio she has little effect on the action of the story, but in a play dominated by men she is nevertheless an eloquent character. She helps us to take her husband's measure. We see her in only two scenes, but her death strikes a remarkable note.

As Brutus plots the assassination, he disregards Portia's intuitive reservations—she knows that something is terribly wrong, though he refuses to tell her what it is (he promises her that he will confide in her later), at his own spiritual peril.

Portia is, as she reminds Brutus, the daughter of the philosopher Cato. This implies that she has inherited some of her father's wisdom. Cato was also an ally of Pompey and enemy of Caesar. Cato committed suicide when Caesar defeated Pompey in civil war. (In the final act of *Julius Caesar*, significantly, Cato the philosopher's son dies in battle. The war Brutus set off has wiped out the philosopher's line. Shakespeare surely intends the symbolism here.)

I HAVE A MAN'S MIND, BUT A WOMAN'S MIGHT

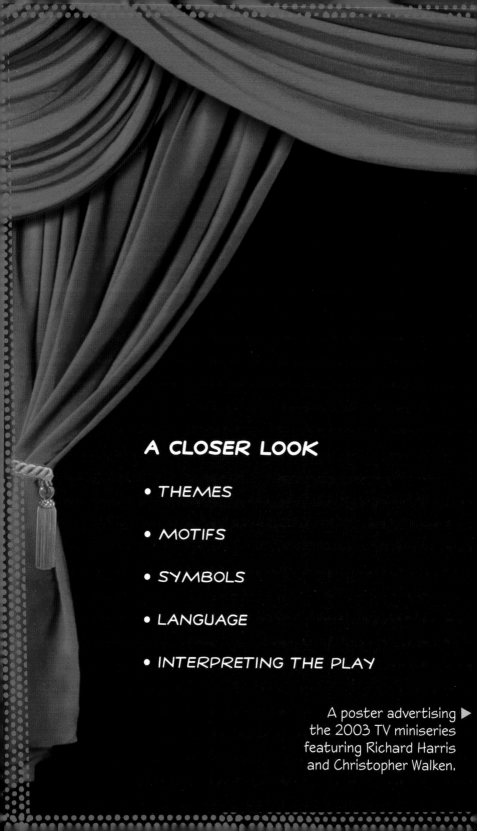

A CLOSER LOOK

- THEMES

- MOTIFS

- SYMBOLS

- LANGUAGE

- INTERPRETING THE PLAY

A poster advertising ▶
the 2003 TV miniseries
featuring Richard Harris
and Christopher Walken.

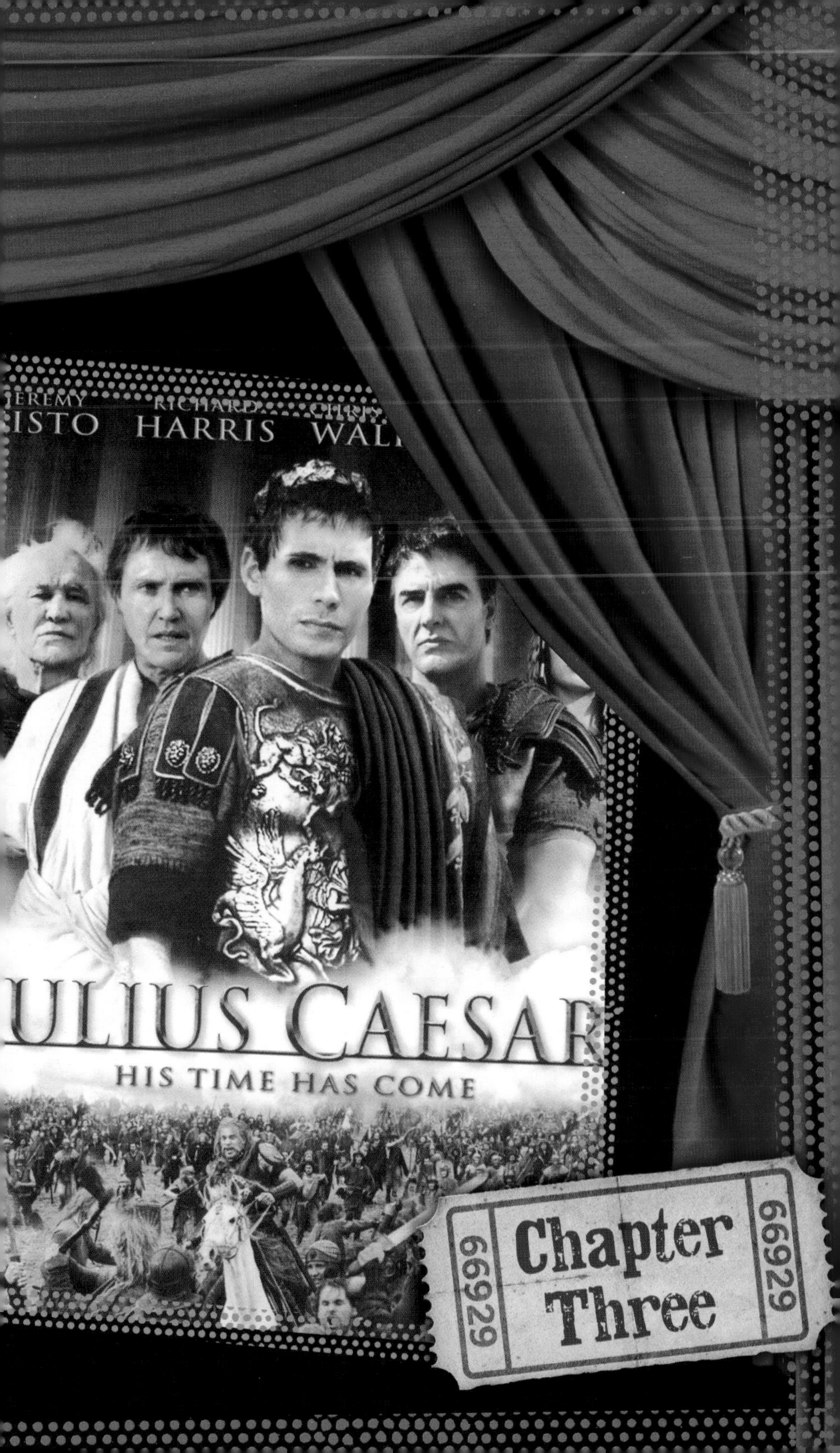

Chapter Three

a Closer Look

THEMES

DANGERS TO REPUBLICAN GOVERNMENT

Brutus fears that Caesar will restore the ancient monarchy by making himself king and destroying the republic. This fear has ties with a well-known legend.

The Romans believed that almost 500 years earlier the self-proclaimed King Tarquin the Proud had committed many atrocities. Shakespeare had treated the evils of Tarquin's rule before, in his long and very great poem, *The Rape of Lucrece*, usually overlooked. According to legend, led by Lucius Junius Brutus, forefather of Marcus Brutus, the people of Rome were roused to fury against the whole ruling family of the Tarquins, who were forced to leave the city.

Once Brutus's ancestor had expelled the Tarquins from Rome, monarchy was abolished. The people of Rome then established a republic, with elected officials representing the various segments of the population, including senators and tribunes.

This is the background against which Shakespeare's Brutus is acting when he thinks Julius Caesar is usurping power and trying to make himself a new king of Rome. He fears that representative government will be destroyed and replaced by the dictatorial rule of Caesar. Such tyranny, he persuades himself, must be stamped out in its earliest beginnings. So he succumbs to the allure of violence. He cannot see any way to preserve the Roman republic other than through violence. Shakespeare shows this to be one of the flaws in Brutus's character. In any case, violence fails to save republican liberty.

THE CORRUPTING NATURE OF VIOLENCE

The apparent theme of *Julius Caesar* is the battle between liberty and slavery; at least that is what its characters keep talking about. But at a deeper level the play asks whether men can resort to violence without themselves becoming enslaved and finally destroyed by it.

With the best will in the world, Brutus reluctantly joins the conspiracy to kill his dear friend Caesar in the hope of keeping Romans free. He achieves the opposite result. Killing Caesar produces a chaos in which freedom and law are lost and the worst elements prevail, as when rioters murder the poet Cinna immediately after Antony's high-sounding speech and, later, when Cato, the philosopher's son, dies in the general slaughter of war. Along the way we learn that even the great statesman Cicero, who has tried to stay aloof from low politics, has been marked for death in the conspirators' remorseless purge of suspected enemies. Nobody is safe.

It is all too reminiscent of the atrocities committed by modern states in the name of "security." The plot of *Julius Caesar* has lost none of its pertinence to our world. The questions it raises will always remain controversial. The world seems determined to keep generating parallel situations: assassinations, civil wars, wily propaganda, bitter clashes of public opinion, attacks on imagined public enemies, and of course an inexhaustible supply of well-meaning fools who suppose that a little more bloodletting can remedy the evils that beset us. Everyone can find their own analogies.

MOTIFS

The men of *Julius Caesar* are competing for glory, for lasting fame. They are public men striking dignified poses as if they were statues (a frequent image in the play). Their speech is highly oratorical and aphoristic, fit to be chiseled on marble monuments. (There are also humble poses: Portia kneels to Brutus, Brutus to Caesar, and Antony's servant to Brutus.)

Caesar hopes and expects to enjoy eternal fame. His killers, similarly, think they will be remembered as great Roman heroes; even the self-effacing Brutus is caught up in the heady spirit of the moment, exulting that he and his fellow conspirators will always be renowned as "the men that gave their country liberty." He and Cassius both foresee their "lofty scene" celebrated in the world's theaters in the distant future.

These very public men hardly have private lives. Caesar and Brutus are the only men who seem to have wives in the play, and both ignore their wives' advice, after which the two women do not appear again. We never learn whether Antony is married. Cassius is married to Brutus's sister, but we are told nothing at all about her (the only glancing reference to this relation is so slight that it is seldom even noticed). The others all seem to be bachelors, for all we know about them.

This is Shakespeare's most masculine play, with only two female characters, both of whom are completely subordinate to the men. This in itself is remarkable, for in his other plays Shakespeare created an amazing range of strong, resourceful women: the sweet Juliet, the witty Beatrice, the shrewish Kate, the ruthless Lady Macbeth, the infinitely fascinating Cleopatra, and dozens of others, all distinct from one another. No man has ever portrayed the opposite sex with such versatility; this time it is as if he has suspended one of the most striking features of his creative genius, in order to depict the interaction of men without the distractions of sex and romance. Again and again men profess their mutual "love."

In this testosterone-fueled work, full of reason and rhetoric, the chief characters, all calculating men, disregard the warnings of soothsayers, dreams, omens, prophecies, and women's intuitions. Caesar and Brutus both ignore their intuitive wives who try to dissuade them from the courses they are determined to follow. These men take for granted that things can be settled by raw power, belittling spiritual influences. This turns out to be a grave error.

Only the cunning Antony seems not to aspire to glory. He is a peerless political improviser, and the purpose of his great speech is purely disruptive: He wants to defame Brutus and the other plotters, bringing the wrath of the plebeians on them.

SYMBOLS

In *Julius Caesar* blood, symbolizing death, flows freely over the stones of Rome. It is neither the hot, youthful blood of *Romeo and Juliet*, the infected and poisoned blood of *Hamlet*, nor the thick, sticky blood of *Macbeth*, but a cold, cleansing, almost impersonal fluid of monumental mortality.

As these Romans vie for fame and honor, we receive a curious impression of cold-bloodedness. Nowhere is this stronger than in Brutus's oration explaining why Caesar had to be slain. But this impression is suddenly dispelled when Antony speaks. *His* blood, at any rate, is boiling. We have already had hints of his warm nature: In contrast to both Brutus and Cassius, he loves games, sports, plays, and other common amusements, and he "revels long o' nights." He is a scrapper. He comes to fight.

Fittingly one of the dominant symbols of *Julius Caesar* is the sword, the instrument of conquest. We hear of the sword, or dagger, (and the hands that wield them) every few lines, until at last Brutus and Cassius stab themselves with the very weapons they used to destroy Caesar.

Death in this play comes publicly, by stabbing and wounds, not by age, sickness, and decay. We hear of butchery, carving, and hewing as the fatal blades flash. Even statues bleed. Cassius uses his dagger, Brutus his "cursed steel," warriors in the sky drizzle blood on Rome, and Casca points to the rising sun with his sword.

LANGUAGE

We would naturally expect a Shakespearean play about ancient Rome to abound in Roman mythology, but there is almost none of that in *Julius Caesar*. The modern reader needs fewer footnotes to follow this play than any other that Shakespeare ever wrote. One passage refers to Virgil's *Aeneid* as if it were genuine history, and another makes a short reference to the "great flood" of which, according to myth, the only survivors were Deucalion and his wife, Pyrrha; there is also a mention of the legendary Colossus of Rhodes, and one of Erebus, the dark region adjoining Hades. However, Shakespeare's usual loving references to the *Metamorphoses* of the Roman poet Ovid, so numerous in his other plays, are entirely absent. Because the play is set in the pagan era, Shakespeare's usual biblical echoes are absent, too.

We might also expect a dense vocabulary, full of long words derived from *Hamlet*, *Macbeth*, or *Troilus and Cressida*, but most of the language of *Julius Caesar* is memorably plain and pithy English, as in "He thinks too much"; "The fault, dear Brutus, is not in our stars"; "Not that I loved Caesar less, but that I loved Rome more"; "If you have tears, prepare to shed them now"; and "This was the noblest Roman of them all." Never did Shakespeare show how eloquent mere monosyllables can be. (So familiar are these phrases that an old joke has a spectator complaining after seeing a performance that *Julius Caesar* consists entirely of clichés.)

The grammar and syntax of *Julius Caesar* are also simple and clear. Shakespeare's later plays are full of language that, in both vocabulary and grammar, seems to defy us to grasp more than a fraction of its meaning on a first hearing. As a storm rages over him, to take a random example, King Lear cries out:

LET THE GREAT GODS, THAT KEEP THIS DREADFUL PUDDERR O'ER OUR HEADS, FIND OUT THEIR ENEMIES NOW. TREMBLE, THOU WRETCH THAT HAST WITHIN THEE UNDIVULGED CRIMES UNWHIPPED OF JUSTICE; HIDE THEE, THOU BLOODY HAND, THOU PERJURED AND THOU SIMULAR MAN OF VIRTUE THAT ART INCESTUOUS; CAITIFF, TO PIECES SHAKE, THAT UNDER COVERT AND CONVENIENT SEEMING HAST PRACTICED ON MAN'S LIFE; CLOSE PENT-UP GUILTS, RIVE YOUR CONCEALING CONTINENTS AND CRY THESE DREADFUL SUMMONERS GRACE. I AM A MAN MORE SINNED AGAINST THAN SINNING.

This is difficult to understand, even baffling, and it is meant to be. Contrast it with Cassius's perfectly lucid explanation of why he resents Caesar's dominance:

> WHY, MAN, HE DOTH BESTRIDE THE NARROW WORLD
> LIKE A COLOSSUS, AND WE PETTY MEN
> WALK UNDER HIS HUGE LEGS AND PEEP ABOUT
> TO FIND OURSELVES DISHONORABLE GRAVES.
> MEN AT SOME TIME ARE MASTERS OF THEIR FATES.
> THE FAULT, DEAR BRUTUS, IS NOT IN OUR STARS
> BUT IN OURSELVES, THAT WE ARE UNDERLINGS.

These two passages suggest the range of styles Shakespeare could command. In *Julius Caesar*, he chooses to use one that makes few difficult demands on readers and spectators.

Morally abstract words dominate the play's conversation, especially *noble*, *honor*, and *virtue*. We feel that the characters are incessantly paying tribute to one another and advertising their own high motives—until Antony suddenly gives the word *honorable* a lethal irony with his sardonic praise of Brutus, over and over again, as an "honorable man." (He repeats the word *honorable* nine times in his speech.) This attack is so deadly that one might almost say that the word has never fully recovered from the way Shakespeare lets Antony keep scourging Brutus with it. Among literate people, it has become hard to call someone "an honorable man" with a straight face: The listener is too apt to hear sarcasm in the phrase.

As a rule Shakespeare's plays are rich in images of animals. Though there are relatively few of them in *Julius Caesar*, the one most often mentioned is a beast of prey, the lion. A lion ominously appears in the streets of Rome, frightening Casca; a lioness also gives birth in the street. Cassius likens Caesar to a lion that preys on the Romans because he finds them as timid as hinds (deer). Caesar himself boasts that he is a lion:

> DANGER KNOWS FULL WELL
> THAT CAESAR IS MORE DANGEROUS THAN HE.
> WE ARE TWO LIONS LITTERED IN ONE DAY,
> AND I THE ELDER AND MORE TERRIBLE.

Caesar is also said to be a wolf preying on sheep.

Animals in Rome are behaving strangely. Owls, nocturnal birds of prey, shriek and hoot in the marketplace at midday. Horses neigh madly. These, like the ghosts, ghastly women, and dead men walking in the streets, are all signs of some terrible event.

INTERPRETING THE PLAY

Julius Caesar deals with real people and events in history, so it can never be wholly separated from related controversies about the past—disputes both ancient and modern.

To judge by every surviving indication, *Julius Caesar* was very popular from the start. Thomas Platter, a Swiss visitor to London, wrote of having seen the play performed in September 1599. Several other references to it at about the same time confirm that it was well known. Dating Shakespeare's plays is always a tricky business, but *Julius Caesar* was certainly a success in the theater before 1600.

The play was first published in the First Folio of 1623; as far as we know, it never appeared in a separate quarto edition, but the Folio text looks very good and presents few problems for scholars and editors.

It is fascinating to contrast Shakespeare's judgment of Brutus and

Cassius with that of the great Italian poet Dante Alighieri. In his immortal poem *The Divine Comedy*—an account of a tour of hell, purgatory, and heaven—Dante condemns Brutus and Cassius to the lowest place in hell, with Judas Iscariot, to be eternally devoured by Satan. For Dante the pair are, like Judas, guilty of the betrayal of a friend and benefactor. Dante regards this as the worst of all sins.

For Shakespeare the assassination of Caesar is far less odious than that, especially on Brutus's side. If Caesar was guilty of subverting the Roman republic and seeking to make himself an unconstitutional monarch, his overthrow may have been justified, or at least defensible.

Modern productions of Shakespeare's play have often been more or less sympathetic to the conspirators. In some, such as Orson Welles's famous 1937 Broadway staging, Caesar was shown as a fascist ruler like Mussolini, and Brutus (played by the young Welles, then only twenty-two years old) was shown as a muddled, well-meaning liberal.

Both the history and the play are oddly intertwined with American history. The great actor Junius Brutus Booth was named after Junius Brutus, the legendary vanquisher of the Tarquins, whom Shakespeare's Brutus (and his real-life model in Plutarch's histories) claimed as an ancestor. One of Booth's several actor sons, John Wilkes Booth, the killer of Abraham Lincoln, played Shakespeare's Brutus on the stage; Lincoln very likely saw him in the role (and in other Shakespearean roles). When Booth shot Lincoln he saw himself as a Brutus saving the American republic from a usurping Caesar. Extreme as this may now sound to us, it belongs to what was once the prevalent American interpretation of the play, which viewed Brutus as a savior of republican government against self-aggrandizing monarchists.

A curious feature of *Julius Caesar* is that Shakespeare departs from all the ancient sources of the story—Plutarch, Appian, and Suetonius. They all report that Brutus was rumored to be Caesar's bastard son, the result of a love affair between Caesar and Brutus's mother, Servilia.

This fact in itself could have furnished the premise of a fascinating play, but Shakespeare never mentions it or even hints at it. Instead he has chosen to write a *political* play, without such rich private motivations complicating its plot about public men striving for power.

In his rebuttal to Brutus, Antony implies that Caesar's killers, despite the lofty reasons they claimed for the act, were driven by their "private griefs"; in his mind, politics is always personal. This is why the play still grips us. But it also raises issues especially close to the hearts of Americans, who trace the birth of their "republican form of government," as the U.S. Constitution calls it, to their rejection of British monarchical rule in 1776.

Like so many of Shakespeare's tragedies, *Julius Caesar* shows the ultimate futility of force and violence in human affairs. The "spirit of Caesar" is more than a ghost; it is the spirit of power, conquest, and domination. Brutus succumbs to the delusion that he can defeat Caesar's spirit by Caesar's means.

Cassius and the others never question this. They assume that violence and treachery are the only ways to achieve anything in politics, whereas before his seduction, Brutus believes in appealing to men's better natures by reason and persuasion.

Brutus's oratory, though intelligent on the surface, proves uninspiring when he tries to justify the bloody methods to which he has resorted. He is essentially too good for politics, which is why, paradoxically, he is no good

ET TU, BRUTE? THEN FALL, CAESAR!

at politics. A man like Antony lives at the passionate level of the plebeians and instinctively understands them far better than Brutus ever can. By sharing and expressing their feelings, the "plain blunt man" controls them like a puppeteer and moves them to a fury that is indeed uncontrollable.

The shrewd Cassius, the "great observer" of men, knows what to expect when Antony goes to work on a mob at such an explosive moment; nobody would ever accuse him of being too good for politics!

Julius Caesar has less vivid and memorable poetic imagery than most of Shakespeare's plays. Its characters seem to prefer formal oratory and rhetoric to lyrical and metaphorical expressions of their personal feelings. They use language much more to persuade other men than to expose their own emotions, except on rare occasions such as when Brutus asks the gods to make him worthy of Portia, a moment of deep and genuine sentiment that tells us how much he must miss her after her death. He is the only character in the play who makes our hearts ache for him, yet this is not typical of *Julius Caesar*.

King Lear and *Othello* have some of the most tear-inducing scenes in all of literature; *Julius Caesar*, however, features more irony than grief. Its subject is not private sorrow, but the frustrations of men in public life.

We never see, for example, the widowed Calpurnia mourning her husband's loss. By the time of Caesar's killing, she has utterly vanished from the story, and we are never even reminded of her again. She does not really exist for her own sake; she is of interest only as a dramatic device, like the Soothsayer and Artemidorus. Her sole function, like theirs, is to try to prevent Caesar from going to the Capitol on the fatal day. Shakespeare keeps our minds fixed on the simple question: Will Caesar keep his appointment with death and destiny? Shakespeare is above all a dramatist who, whatever else he does, must always keep us in suspense.

None of Shakespeare's plays contains less laughter than *Julius Caesar*. One can hardly believe that this drama is the work of the same playwright who created the hilarious Falstaff and the bewitching Cleopatra. The play is also nearly devoid of music, rhyme, and other typical elements of Shakespeare's work. Even in *Othello*, an unremittingly serious tragedy, a clown and some musicians make a brief appearance, and a comical Porter relieves the horror of *Macbeth*. Shakespeare seems to want each of his plays to differ from all the others in some striking respect; he is never content to repeat his successes. If he uses a formula, he uses it with some notable variation from his previous ventures to surprise our expectations.

"AY, CAESAR, BUT NOT GONE."

Chronology

1564 William Shakespeare is born on April 23 in Stratford-upon-Avon, England

1578-1582 Span of Shakespeare's "Lost Years," covering the time between leaving school and marrying Anne Hathaway of Stratford

1582 At age eighteen Shakespeare marries Anne Hathaway, age twenty-six, on November 28

1583 Susanna Shakespeare, William and Anne's first child, is born in May, six months after the wedding

1584 Birth of twins Hamnet and Judith Shakespeare

1585-1592 Shakespeare leaves his family in Stratford to become an actor and playwright in a London theater company

1587 Public beheading of Mary Queen of Scots

1593-94 The Bubonic (Black) Plague closes theaters in London

1594-96 As a leading playwright, Shakespeare creates some of his most popular work, including *A Midsummer Night's Dream* and *Romeo and Juliet*

1596 Hamnet Shakespeare dies in August at age eleven, possibly of plague

1596–97	*The Merchant of Venice* and *Henry IV, Part One* most likely are written
1599	The Globe Theater opens
1600	*Julius Caesar* is first performed at the Globe
1600–01	*Hamlet* is believed to have been written
1601–02	*Twelfth Night* is probably composed
1603	Queen Elizabeth dies; Scottish king James VI succeeds her and becomes England's James I
1604	Shakespeare pens *Othello*
1605	*Macbeth* is composed
1608–1610	London's theaters are forced to close when the plague returns and kills an estimated 33,000 people
1611	*The Tempest* is written
1613	The Globe Theater is destroyed by fire
1614	Reopening of the Globe
1616	Shakespeare dies on April 23
1623	Anne Hathaway, Shakespeare's widow, dies; a collection of Shakespeare's plays, known as the First Folio, is published

Source Notes

p. 38, par. 1, Bradley, A.C. *Shakespearean Tragedy.* (New York: Penguin, 1991). Bradley's lectures on *Hamlet, Othello, King Lear,* and *Macbeth* have gone back to press many times in the past century and have been enjoyed by generations of Shakespeare enthusiasts.

p. 40, par. 3, Gaius Suetonius Tranquillus, *The Twelve Caesars (Penguin Classics).* (New York: Penguin, 2003).

p. 41, par. 1, The prologue to *The Rape of Lucrece* is available at The Literature Network, http://www.online-literature.com/shakespeare/331/

p. 51, par. 6, Lupercalia was celebrated on February 15 and involved elaborate rituals thought to enhance fertility and purification. For a brief description of the rites and their historical connection with Mark Antony and events leading to Caesar's death, see http://penelope.uchicago.edu/~grout/encyclopaedia_romana/calendar/lupercalia.html

p. 55, par. 4, Plutarch describes Caesar's assassination in his *Lives,* a collection of biographies of ancient Greek and Roman heroes and villains. Read the account at http://bostonleadershipbuilders.com/plutarch/caesar.htm

p. 73, par. 2, Sister Miriam Joseph. *Shakespeare's Use of the Arts of Language.* (Philadelphia: Paul Dry Books, 2005).This classic 1947 work is back in print and remains an invaluable guide for students of rhetoric as well as of Shakespeare.

p. 81, par. 1, In Act I, scene 1 of *Hamlet,* the ghost of the dead King Hamlet appears to the sentinels on the castle's ramparts. Shakespeare sets up terrific dramatic tension within the first fifty lines, and in less than two hundred lines he takes us from midnight to dawn, manipulating our sense of time with astounding skill.

p. 95, par. 4, Jean Renoir (1894-1979), son of Impressionist painter Pierre-Auguste Renoir, spoke these lines as the character Octave in his 1939 film *La Régle du Jeu (The Rules of the Game)* : "You see, in this world, there is one awful thing, and that is that everyone has his reasons."

A Shakespeare Glossary

The student should not try to memorize these, but only refer to them as needed. We can never stress enough that the best way to learn Shakespeare's language is simply to *hear* it—to hear it spoken well by good actors. After all, small children master every language on earth through their ears, without studying dictionaries, and we should master Shakespeare, as much as possible, the same way.

addition —a name or title (knight, duke, duchess, king, etc.)

admire —to marvel

affect —to like or love; to be attracted to

an —if ("An I tell you that, I'll be hanged.")

approve —to prove or confirm

attend —to pay attention

belike —probably

beseech —to beg or request

betimes —soon; early

bondman —a slave

bootless —futile; useless; in vain

broil —a battle

charge —expense, responsibility; to command or accuse

clepe, clept —to name; named

common —of the common people; below the nobility

conceit —imagination

condition —social rank; quality

countenance —face; appearance; favor

cousin —a relative

cry you mercy —beg your pardon

curious —careful; attentive to detail

dear —expensive

discourse —to converse; conversation

discover —to reveal or uncover

dispatch —to speed or hurry; to send; to kill

doubt —to suspect

entreat —to beg or appeal

envy —to hate or resent; hatred; resentment

ere —before

ever, e'er —always

eyne —eyes

fain —gladly

fare —to eat; to prosper

favor —face, privilege

fellow —a peer or equal

filial —of a child toward its parent

fine —an end; in fine = in sum

fond —foolish

fool —a darling

genius —a good or evil spirit

gentle —well-bred; not common;

gentleman —one whose labor was done by servants (Note: to
     call someone a *gentleman* was not a mere compliment on his
     manners; it meant that he was above the common people.)

gentles —people of quality

get —to beget (a child)

go to —"go on"; "come off it"

go we —let us go

haply —perhaps

happily —by chance; fortunately

hard by —nearby

heavy —sad or serious

husbandry —thrift; economy

instant —immediate

kind —one's nature; species

knave —a villain; a poor man

lady —a woman of high social rank (Note: *lady* was not a synonym for *woman* or *polite woman*; it was not a compliment, but, like *gentleman*, simply a word referring to one's actual legal status in society.)

leave — permission; "take my leave" = depart (with permission)

lief, lieve —"I had as lief" = I would just as soon; I would rather

like —to please; "it likes me not" = it is disagreeable to me

livery —the uniform of a nobleman's servants; emblem

mark —notice; pay attention

morrow —morning

needs —necessarily

nice —too fussy or fastidious

owe —to own

passing —very

peculiar —individual; exclusive

privy —private; secret

proper —handsome; one's very own ("his proper son")

protest —to insist or declare

quite —completely

require —request

several —different, various;

severally —separately

sirrah —a term used to address social inferiors

sooth —truth

state —condition; social rank

still —always; persistently

success —result(s)

surfeit —fullness

touching —concerning; about; as for

translate —to transform

unfold —to disclose

villain —a low or evil person; originally, a peasant

voice —a vote; consent; approval

vouchsafe —to confide or grant

vulgar —common

want —to lack

weeds —clothing

what ho —"hello, there!"

wherefore —why

wit —intelligence; sanity

withal —moreover; nevertheless

without —outside

would —wish

Suggested Essay Topics

1. Does *Julius Caesar* have a villain? Who is most responsible for the evil in the story?

2. How might the play have been different if Brutus were identified, as in Shakespeare's historical sources, as Caesar's illegitimate son?

3. Caesar and Brutus both ignore their wives' misgivings and advice, as well as supernatural omens. How does this affect the outcome of events?

4. Before Julius Caesar, Rome was a republic, ruled by the Senate and various officers who had limited powers. After him, it was ruled by all-powerful emperors, called "Caesars." The surname had become a title; a revolution had occurred. Discuss what this tells us about the conspirators' aim of saving the Roman republic from Julius Caesar's alleged monarchical ambition.

5. Do the characters of *Julius Caesar* remind you of any figures in American politics today? What do you think Shakespeare would have thought of modern democracy?

Testing Your Memory

1. At the beginning of the play, the common people are celebrating the defeat of whom? a) Julius Caesar; b) Pompey the Great; c) Lucius Junius Brutus; d) Caius Ligarius.

2. What has Mark Antony offered Caesar? a) a sword; b) an olive branch; c) a crown; d) his daughter's hand in marriage.

3. What is Caesar's wife's affliction? a) sterility; b) poverty; c) ambition; d) the plague.

4. Caesar's wife is a) Cleopatra; b) Portia; c) Calpurnia; d) Octavia.

5. How are Brutus and Cassius related? They are a) old enemies; b) cousins; c) classmates; d) brothers-in-law.

6. Who is Cicero? a) a gladiator; b) a chariot driver; c) a tribune of the people; d) an orator.

7. Who is Lucius? a) a conspirator; b) Brutus's servant; c) a gladiator; d) an orator.

8. Who is Portia's father? a) Caesar; b) Brutus; c) Cato; d) Metellus Cimber.

9. Calpurnia dreams of a) an earthquake; b) lions in the streets; c) a murder; d) civil war.

10. The conspirators persuade Caesar to come to the Capitol by a) threatening him; b) playing on his vanity; c) enlisting Antony's help; d) winning Calpurnia's support.

11. To what heavenly body does Caesar liken himself? a) the sun; b) the moon; c) Ursa Major; d) the North Star.

12. Who is the first to stab Caesar? a) Casca; b) Brutus; c) Cassius; d) Cimber.

13. Antony promises every Roman citizen a) money; b) glory; c) freedom; d) peace.

14. Cinna the poet is killed by a) Cinna the conspirator; b) a mob; c) Casca; d) accident.

15. Julius Caesar's nephew is a) Lucius; b) Romulus; c) Remus; d) Octavius.

16. What happens to Cicero under the new regime? a) he receives new honors; b) he is put to death; c) his writings are publicly burned; d) he is paid for his services.

17. Who was Marcus Brutus's famous ancestor? a) Titus Andronicus; b) Caius Marcius Coriolanus; c) Lucius Junius Brutus; d) Cominius.

18. Brutus accuses Cassius of a) murder; b) treason; c) feigning illness; d) taking bribes.

19. Where does Caesar's ghost say he will meet Brutus? a) at Philippi; b) at Rome; c) in Hades; d) in Athens.

20. Cassius dies on a) the Ides of March ; b) his birthday; c) the anniversary of the assassination; d) a Roman holiday.

Answer Key

14. b; 15. d; 16. b; 17. c; 18. d; 19. a; 20. b

1. b; 2. c; 3. a; 4. c; 5. d; 6. d; 7. b; 8. c; 9. c; 10. b; 11. d; 12. a; 13. a;

Further Information

BOOKS

Ackroyd, Peter. *Shakespeare: The Biography*. New York: Nan A. Talese, 2005.

Dunton-Downer, Leslie, and Alan Riding. *The Essential Shakespeare Handbook*. New York: Dorling-Kindersley, 2004.

Folger Shakespeare Library *Julius Caesar*. New York: Washington Square Press, 2004.

Shakespeare's Julius Caesar (The Manga Edition). Hoboken, NJ: Wiley Publishing, 2008.

WEB SITES

Absolute Shakespeare is a resource for the Bard's plays, sonnets, and poems and includes summaries, quotes, films, trivia, and more. http://absoluteshakespeare.com

Play Shakespeare: The Ultimate Free Shakespeare Resource features all the play texts with an online glossary, reviews, a discussion forum, and links to festivals worldwide. http://www.playshakespeare.com

William Shakespeare Info: *Julius Caesar* provides a vast collection of links related to the specific play, as well as articles about Shakespeare's life, world, and work. http://www.william-shakespeare.info/shakespeare-play-julius-caesar.htm

FILMS

Julius Caesar was a popular 1953 MGM film, directed by Joseph L. Mankiewicz and featuring a fine all-star cast: Louis Calhern as Caesar, James Mason as Brutus, Marlon Brando as Antony, John Gielgud as Cassius, Greer Garson as Calpurnia, and Deborah Kerr as Portia. This was the only Shakespearean role of Brando's career; Gielgud's brilliant performance as Cassius was already legendary on the British stage.

Julius Caesar was remade in 1970 with another all-star cast, this time starring John Gielgud as Caesar himself. Charlton Heston delivered a strong Mark Antony and Jason Robards played Brutus. Other roles include Diana Rigg (Portia) and Robert Vaughn (Casca).

AUDIO BOOK

Julius Caesar (Arkangel Shakespeare), BBC Audiobooks America; performed by Michael Feast, Adrian Lester, and the Arkangel cast.

RECORDING

Julius Caesar has been recorded many times. One of the finest recordings was directed by Howard Sackler in 1964, with an excellent cast headed by Anthony Quayle as Brutus, Ralph Richardson as Caesar, and Alan Bates as Antony.

Bibliography

General Commentary

Bate, Jonathan, and Eric Rasmussen, eds. *William Shakespeare Complete Works (Modern Library)*. New York: Random House, 2007.

Bloom, Harold. *Shakespeare: The Invention of the Human*. New York: Riverhead Books,1998.

Garber, Marjorie. *Shakespeare After All*. New York: Pantheon, 2004.

Goddard, Harold C. *The Meaning of Shakespeare*. Chicago: University of Chicago Press, 1951.

Traversi, D. L. *An Approach to Shakespeare*. Palo Alto, CA: Stanford University Press, 1957.

Van Doren, Mark. *Shakespeare*. Garden City, NY: Doubleday, 1939.

Biography

Burgess, Anthony. *Shakespeare*. New York: Alfred A. Knopf, 1970.

Chute, Marchette. *Shakespeare of London*. New York: Dutton, 1949.

Greenblatt, Stephen. *Will in the World: How Shakespeare Became Shakespeare*. New York: W. W. Norton & Company, 2004.

Honan, Park. *Shakespeare: A Life*. New York: Oxford University Press, 1998.

Schoenbaum, Samuel. *William Shakespeare: A Documentary Life*. New York: Oxford University Press, 1975.

———. *William Shakespeare: Records and Images*. New York: Oxford University Press, 1981.

Index

Page numbers in **boldface** are illustrations.

a

Act I
  scene 1, 44–45
  scene 2, 45–47, 49
  scene 3, 49–51
Act II
  scene 1, 51–56
  scene 2, 56–58
  scene 3, 58
  scene 4, 59
Act III
  scene 1, 59, 61, 63–66
  scene 2, 66–74
  scene 3, 74–75
Act IV
  scene 1, 75–76
  scene 2, 76–77
  scene 3, 77–81
Act V
  scene 1, 81–82
  scene 2, 82–83
  scene 3, 83–85
  scene 4, 85–86
  scene 5, 86-87
actors and acting, 4, 12, 21
animal imagery, 106–107
authorship, doubts about, 24–25

B

Bacon, Francis, 24
Booth, John Wilkes, 108
Bradley, A. C., 38
Brutus, 41, 92–94

Burbage, Richard, 12

C

Calpurnia, 110–111
Cassius, 40, 41, 95–96
characters, 5, 28, 39–40, 88, 89–97, 103
comedies, 5, 26, 29

D

Dante Alighieri, 108
de Vere, Edward, Earl of Oxford, 25
diseases, 18, 21

E

education, 12
Elizabeth I, 11, **18**, 40
entertainment, 18–23
epitaph, Shakespeare's, 30

F

family life, 10–12, 26, 30, 102
famous phrases, 5, 9, 38, 105
Fiennes, Joseph, **27**
Fiennes, Ralph, **72**
folio editions, 30, 107

G

Garson, Greer, **54**
Gibson, Mel, 14

Globe Theater, 20, **20**, 22
glossaries, 32–35, 115–118
government, 100–101
grammar and syntax, 105–106
Greatrex, Christina, **48**
groundlings, 19

H

Hamlet, 13–14, 28
Hamlet (character), 5, 92
Hathaway, Anne, 12, 30
Hayes, James, **62**
Henry IV, Part One, 14
Henry VI, 23
heroes, tragic, 39–40, 89–90, 91
historical sources, 108–109
history plays, 5, 23, 26
Hogg, Ian, **65**

I

interpretations, of *Julius Caesar*,
   107–111

J

Jacobi, Derek, 13
Johnson, Ben, 31
Julius Caesar (character), 89–91
Julius Caesar (historical figure), 40

K

Kerr, Deborah, **54**
King Lear, 29, 105
King's Men, 28–29

L

language, Shakespearean, 5, 6–8,
   9–10, 104–107, 110
Lincoln, Abraham, 108
literary references, 6, 104
literary terms, glossary of, 32–35
Lord Chamberlain's Men, 12

M

Macbeth, 14–15, 29, 111
Mannion, Tom, **65**
Mark Antony, 94–95
Marlowe, Christopher, 25
Mason, Brewster, **48**
The Merchant of Venice, 15
Meres, Francis, 26
A Midsummer Night's Dream, 5, 15
motifs, 102–103
movies, 8, 13–17

O

Olivier, Laurence, 13
Othello, 16, 29, 111

P

Pigott-Smith, Tim, **67**
plays, 13–17, 20, 22–23, 26–28
plots, sources of, 40, 108–109
poems, 5, 12, 29–30
Portia, 97
Puritans, 19, 21–22

Q

quarto editions, 23

R

The Rape of Lucrece, 12, 100
relevance, modern, 101–102
religion, 10–11, 18–19, 28
republic, Roman, 100–101
reputation, Shakespeare's, 4, 27, 31
Richard III, 23
Romeo and Juliet, 16, 26

S

sarcasm, 106
Shakespeare, William
childhood home of, **11**
doubts about authorship, 24–25
early life, 10–12
family life, 12, 26
grave of, **30**
later life and death of, 28–30
reputation of, 4, 27, 31
Shakespearean Tragedy (Bradley), 38
Shakespeare in Love (movie), **27**
soliloquies, 39
sonnets, 29–30
spectators, 19, 21
symbols, 103–104

T

The Taming of the Shrew, 23, 26
The Tempest, 17, 29
10 Things I Hate About You (movie), 23
Testing Your Memory, 120–121

theater, Elizabethan, 18–23
themes, 100–102
touring companies, 21
tragedies, 4, 27–28, 29, 38, 39–40
Twelfth Night, 17
The Twelve Caesars (Suetonius), 40
tyrants, 40

V

Venus and Adonis, 12
villains, 95–96
violence, corrupting nature of, 101–102, 109

W

Washington, Denzel, **93**
Welles, Orson, 108
West Side Story (musical), 26
women, 21, 103
word choices, 105, 106

Z

Zeffirelli, Franco, 14, 16

About the Author

Joseph Sobran is the author of several books, including *Alias Shakespeare* (1997). He lives in northern Virginia.